TIME-SAVING TECHNIQUES
FOR BUILDING MODEL RAILROADS

Tony Koester

Kalmbach Media

Acknowledgements

I extend my sincere appreciation to those who provided information and photos, many of whom are listed below. Special thanks are due to Eric Brooman, Jack Burgess, Gregg Condon, Bill Darnaby, Bernie Kempinski, Tom Klimoski, and Doug Tagsold. Others who provided valuable assistance include Joe Atkinson, Ken Browning of Woodland Scenics, Ken Clark, Kip Grant, Jeff Halloin, Bob Hanmer, Frank Hodina, Randy Laframboise, Doug Leffler, Jeff Martin, Allen McClelland, Lance Mindheim, Jeff Otto, Karen Parker, Clark Propst, Neil Schofield, Brooks Stover, Perry Squier, and Rich Taylor. Special thanks are extended to Jeff Wilson, Eric White, Lisa Schroeder, and Diane Bacha, who guided this book through Kalmbach's meticulous production process.

Tony Koester
Newton, N.J.

On the cover:

Doug Tagsold, builder of four railroads in HO, On3, and now this narrow gauge Colorado & Southern in 1:72, is among the experts who share tips on how to build a model railroad more quickly. *Photo by Doug Tagsold*

Kalmbach Media
21027 Crossroads Circle
Waukesha, Wisconsin 53186
www.KalmbachHobbyStore.com

Published in 2019
23 22 21 20 19   1 2 3 4 5

Manufactured in China

ISBN: 978-1-62700-690-3
EISBN: 978-1-62700-691-0

Editor: Jeff Wilson
Book Design: Lisa Schroeder

Library of Congress Control Number: 2018967290

Contents

INTRODUCTION

What's the point?

Modeling a "flatlands" (with lots of bridges!) railroad gave me a chance to apply hard-won lessons—my own and those taught to me by others—about building well but much more quickly. Example: I handlaid a half-dozen turnouts before deciding to use Micro Engineering flextrack and no. 6 turnouts in one yard, modified Shinohara no. 8s on the main, and Central Valley no. 8 tie strips, some curved, in the other yard.

When we think of a hobby, we tend to frame it in terms of a relaxing, leisure-time activity, something akin to puttering around in the garden. That is not what this book is about. I assume the title was a clue: You're a busy guy or gal, you want a scale model railroad on which to operate your trains with some degree of prototypical realism, and you don't have forever and a day to get there from here. How, you wonder, do those who get sizable home layouts built actually do that? In the next 100-odd pages, let's discuss that.

I suspect most readers of this book will be at least vaguely aware of my background. Two aspects of it stand out as far as this book's content is concerned: First, I edited *Railroad Model Craftsman* from 1969 to early 1981, and editing a model railroad magazine put me in contact with most of the hobby's leading movers and shakers. I have edited *Model Railroad Planning*, an annual issue of *Model Railroader*, since it was founded in 1995, which allows me to maintain and grow those contacts.

Second, since we built our home in 1973, I have constructed two large ("basement-size") HO model railroads (see photos at left and right). During that period, I had a busy professional career, first at RMC, then at Bell Laboratories and successor companies (with a 50-mile-each-way commute), and finally working under contract to Kalmbach Media. Judy and I also raised four children and three dogs, and I was a sailplane flight instructor on weekends in the 1970s into the 1980s.

The upshot of this is that if I wanted not one but two operating, fully scenicked model railroads, which I most definitely did, I had to adopt or develop many time-saving techniques. That's what this book is about.

There are many other modelers who have developed time-saving techniques and whose work I have come to respect and admire over the years, and you'll hear from them throughout the book and especially in Chapter 8, "Tips from the masters."

One thing we won't touch on to any degree is short cuts to realistic operation. That's well covered in my book, *Realistic Model Railroad Operation, Second Edition* (Kalmbach, 2013), especially in Chapter 2, a four-page quick-start guide.

Remember that what you read here

The Allegheny Midland—Midland Road—occupied my basement for a quarter century. My priorities were different when I started construction in 1973: handlaid track, mountain scenery, showing that stub-ended ("muzzle-loading") staging yards worked well, and so on. Getting it operational took about seven years.

is a compilation of tips and techniques that worked for me and other veteran modelers. You'll note that setting priorities that put building a layout near the top of the list, often to the exclusion of what you may regard as normal leisure-time activities, is a repeated mantra. As you often see following comments on the internet, YMMV—your mileage may vary.

With that caveat in mind, let's get started.

1 Even master track planner John Armstrong usually went through multiple iterations of a track plan he was preparing for a client (he's shown using an electric eraser). Note the rack of pre-sized curve templates in the corner above the coffee cups. The lesson here is that you can save time by outsourcing some tasks to the professionals, or you can elect to save money at a cost in time by doing things yourself. Usually, a balance between the two is both economical and rewarding. *Paul Dolkos*

CHAPTER ONE

Goals based on time, space, & budget

It's nice to have a clean sheet of paper or computer screen on which to start planning your next layout. It's also a bit terrifying, as there are so many opportunities to explore, reams of knowledge to acquire, and mistakes to be made. Our goal in this book is to find ways to consume fewer resources while building a model railroad—for example, achieving a balance between saving time by spending money, **1**, and vice versa. So let's first examine the variables to see what our options may be.

The first HO railroad I constructed was the basement-size Allegheny Midland. I did virtually all of the work, including handlaying codes 70 and 83 track and turnouts, although brass steam locomotive improvements, repairs, painting, and weathering were outsourced.

Been there, done that

First, let's define "quickly." As I noted in the Introduction, I have built two basement-size railroads since 1973. I spent 25 years building and operating the HO scale Allegheny Midland, **2**, and since about 2000 I have been building and operating an HO depiction of the Nickel Plate Road's St. Louis Division, **3**. Despite working by myself for the most part, both achieved a high degree of completion (few model railroads can be proclaimed "done").

If this seems to you like too long a time span to spend on a model railroad and well beyond the book's premise of "quickly," I have several suggestions. First, make a decision on what you consider reasonable in terms of time and other expenditures before making

grandiose and impractical plans given those constraints.

Second, note that I also built a fully scenicked 1:29 scale project railroad based on a New Hampshire short line for *Model Railroader* in less than a year, **4**. And I built an O scale project railroad based on an Indiana town for a series in MR in 2020 in about the same time frame, **5**.

Third, consider that Doug Tagsold built a basement-size HO model of the Denver & Rio Grande Western's Moffat Tunnel line, a basement-size On3 model of the Rio Grande's Durango-to-Silverton, Colo., line and an HO model based on a belt line around Toledo, Ohio. He's now working on a 1:72 model of the narrow gauge Colorado & Southern (see cover and *Model Railroad Planning* 2018.)

In each case, it took him only one year to reach the operational stage and five years for the scenery to be relatively complete. I can't imagine anyone other than a professional layout builder working full time could make such progress in less time! How does he get so much done? See Chapter 9.

Fourth, Dave Frary, who with Bob Hayden was a highly regarded contributor to RMC during my tenure as editor (1969–1981), **6**, builder of many custom layouts, and author of a best-selling Kalmbach book on making scenery, once shared with me his simple secret to getting so much done: "I get up an hour early to build models before going to work. By doing that everyday, I get a surprising amount of modeling done."

3 My current HO railroad is an accurate, selectively condensed model of the eastern half of the Nickel Plate Road's St. Louis Division in 1954. Friends helped with some wiring and tracklaying in one staging yard; scratchbuilt two depots; and provided a number of freight cars. DCC sound-decoder installation; steam detailing, painting, and weathering; and signaling and interchange-control systems were outsourced.

Getting started

Perhaps the most important lesson to learn is that it's almost mandatory to have an attractive, comfortable, pleasant place to build models and the railroad itself. I've seen more than a few nicely conceived model railroads grind to an early halt because the setting for the new layout wasn't a place we'd normally choose to hang out.

Two examples come to mind: When the late Hal Carstens, publisher of *Railroad Model Craftsman* and other hobby magazines and books, bought an 8-acre lot in northwestern New Jersey as Carstens Publications prepared to move to rural Sussex County in 1973, it came with a dairy barn. Hal, Jim Boyd, and I inspected the hayloft and proclaimed it more than ample for Hal's proposed Susquehanna Northern.

But there was a catch—several of them, in fact: The loft wasn't insulated, heated, or cooled; it had no ceiling or finished walls or flooring; and, perhaps worst of all, it was located quite a long walk downhill from the new house. It would take someone with more motivation than I have to come home from a long day at the office, turn on the loft's heating or cooling system, eat dinner, and then trudge back down to the barn, especially on a cold, dark winter night.

Hal wisely decided instead to use the ample basement in his new home. Despite being a busy business owner, the father of four active children, and engaged in other community activities, he managed to erect all of the benchwork and had laid a lot of track by the time he died. I doubt that would

have happened had he attempted to work in the barn, and the cost of doing so would have been much greater.

RMC's former part-time projects editor, my good friend Bob Mohowski, started construction of an HO edition of the New York, Ontario & Western in his unfinished basement. Again, Bob soon realized that heading down into a poorly lit, dank basement after a day teaching school was not conducive to rapid progress. Time for Plan B: As his two boys grew up and left the nest, he was able to run an HO model of the Pennsylvania Railroad's Elmira Branch between adjoining bedrooms.

That railroad reached fully operational status before he and wife Pat retired and built a new home in upstate New York. The new house has an ample basement—perhaps

4 Former interurban—later short line—Claremont & Concord in New Hampshire was the theme of a 1:29 project railroad I built for *Model Railroader*. It was a pleasant diversion from building the Nickel Plate in HO scale and showed how magazine—or self-imposed—deadlines ensure rapid progress.

too ample, Bob realized. So he is already well along on a new layout in a main-floor room where all the comforts of home are readily available. He relocated to an area replete with active, experienced model railroaders and an active National Model Railroad Division and Region, so there is also skilled and enthusiastic support nearby.

Make mistakes!

Neil Gaiman, author of *American Gods,* offered some very good advice: "It's better to make a hundred mistakes

5 Once again, working against immovable magazine deadlines ensured rapid progress as I built a portable O fine-scale model of a small Indiana town for an upcoming series in MR. Changing scales, even temporarily, provides insights about new ways to tackle tough problems.

than to stare at a blank piece of paper too scared to do anything wrong." Others have similarly suggested we should just do something; mistakes can usually be fixed, and it may turn out okay anyway.

I'll temper this advice by recommending that we should strive to get the underpinnings right the first time. Thin subroadbed may save money initially but turn out to be very expensive in the long run if it has to be shored up (in terms of time) or replaced (time and money). You

wouldn't scrimp on the foundation of your house, so why do so on what could turn out to be one of your most rewarding accomplishments?

We'll chat more about layout design and construction in subsequent chapters.

Model railroaders, as a whole, tend to be inherently frugal, even cheap. We brag about buying used code 100 flextrack (which, in HO, is like using I-beams for rails) at a swap meet without any regard for whether that track will compromise the appearance of our railroads. Replacing that later on with code 70 or increasingly popular code 83 track, which represents heavy-duty but still reasonably sized 132-pound rail, is difficult and expensive, hence seldom done. Better that we started there in the first place.

Overcoming inertia

A problem we all face at one time or another is overcoming inertia. As I mentioned above, the most prolific modelers have discovered that an hour a day allows tremendous progress, mainly by creating a work ethic. A single hour per day at a time when not much else was competing for your

Thatcher's Inlet, an HOn30 layout depicting the Maine seacoast built by Dave Frary and Bob Hayden, was an incredibly popular feature in RMC. They mastered quick but highly effective construction and scenery techniques that were later applied to custom layout construction where time was literally money. *Dave Frary*

attention will achieve wonders.

New Englanders are notoriously tight with a penny, and Frary and Hayden were well known for using inexpensive materials. There's an important secondary lesson here: Saving money often equates to saving time, as we can't move forward on a project for our model railroads if we can't afford the supplies needed to complete them.

There are indeed times when "throwing money" at a project saves time—outsourcing locomotive repair and detailing or decoder installation, perhaps. But there are also times when a lack of funds slows or stops a project's progress as surely as a lack of time or motivation.

Please see Chapter 8 for more tips from several highly experienced model railroaders.

Budgeting resources

The previous discussion leads us to a chat about budgeting. We are advised to create a household budget to be sure we know where our money goes and when it needs to go there. When things aren't working out as we expected, studying the budget usually uncovers expenses that we can trim.

You're not going to have the layout of your dreams within a reasonable timeframe if you don't allocate adequate funding for it. This overview of the east- and westbound yards at Frankfort, Ind., suggests the scope of the investment in rolling stock, most of it plastic kits or ready-to-run models, required to fill the roster

My wife, Judy, and I do a reasonable amount of traveling. Often it's to a rail-related event, but just as often it's to a Bucket List destination with friends we met through the broad-shouldered hobby of model railroading.

True, we may be a little unusual in that regard, as except for 20-plus years at Bell Laboratories and successor companies, most of my career has been spent in the model railroad industry. This in turn led to making a lot of

8 I scratchbuilt—finally—this model of the joint NKP–C&EI depot in Cayuga, Ind. I wasn't sure how to approach constructing this complex brick structure, but once I decided to dive in, it went rather quickly. Many projects look far more intimidating than they actually are, and every mistake is a valuable training exercise.

fellow-hobbyist friends. Unlike me, however, those friends with whom we travel are not veterans of the model railroad industry. Our mutual hobby provides a convenient platform for friendships to grow and prosper.

The point I want to make is that a hobby can become a lifestyle. My life is incredibly richer because of my involvement in our hobby. Judy and I

traveled halfway around the world on several occasions because of our hobby.

This strongly suggests that our hobby can have tremendous value and greatly enhance the enjoyment of our lives. I therefore suggest that hobby expenditures, including hobby-related travel, deserve to be a line item on our household budgets. Like vacations, golf, boats, and other "leisure-time"

activities, model railroading can easily become a very important aspect of the quality of our lives, and those of our non-hobbyist spouses. It would be a shame if funding hobby expenses is regarded as what we do with the change left over in our pockets. That will greatly slow or end progress on building a model railroad, **7**.

Over-thinking things

Perhaps the most common misstep modelers take is to over-think a project. They assume that they don't have enough information or that they don't know how to do thus and so, and they freeze in their tracks.

You are never going to have all of the information you want to have or think you need. Period. If, for example, you get lucky and find scale drawings of a depot you plan to model, are you sure those drawings are accurate? Builders often deviate from the blueprints. Is it correct for the year you're modeling? Early clapboard or novelty siding may have been replaced with board-and-batten, or vice versa. Perhaps it was updated with some

9 When Jack Burgess discovered his first model of the Merced, Calif., depot was somewhat inaccurate, he built the one shown here. But the first depot served its purpose for several years, so no time was wasted, and the scene complemented the railroad.
Jack Burgess

Plans to operate the Allegheny Midland in steam faded because of the lack of accurate, well-detailed, and smooth-running Nickel Plate Road or Chesapeake & Ohio models in the 1970s. Atlas (V&O SD24 and AM GP38) and Athearn (U30B) diesels filled the bill until the mid-1980s when good steam became available.

Choosing an era to model for my Nickel Plate layout was easy: I wanted to capture the last fall grain rush using 2-8-4 Berkshires and 2-8-2 Mikados, employ Alco PA-1s on Cleveland–St. Louis trains 9 and 10, and run Alco RS-3s on Peoria and Toledo Division trains. That narrowed my choices to the fall of 1954, as the RS-3s arrived in early 1954 and steam came off in July 1955.

windows boarded up at a later date, or dormers or ornate trim was removed.

My model of the joint Nickel Plate Road–Chicago & Eastern Illinois depot, **8**, which graced the northwest corner of the level crossing between those two railroads into the 1970s, is an example of part of this problem. I lived in Cayuga during the 1950s and often visited the depot. Two friends and I measured and photographed the depot in the early 1970s, and Julian Cavalier took those field notes and made what seem to be very accurate drawings of it that appeared in the July 1982 RMC.

So I had sufficient information about the prototype. What I didn't have was a good battle plan. The depot has a cranked or compound (two-slope) hip roof, which is no problem to model—until you get to the 90-degree corner. There the roof comprises two overlapping, truncated cones. There are also two full cones, one over each operators' bay window.

I puzzled over this for more than a decade while a foam mock-up to which I attached printouts of photos served as the Cayuga depot. Only when videographer Forrest Nace proposed doing a DVD of the railroad was I finally shamed into diving into the deep end of the pool.

I started building the straight walls as I worked up my courage to tackle the curved corner wall and bay windows. Step by step, I kept plowing ahead, occasionally retracing my steps to correct something that wasn't working out as well as I had hoped. Sometimes I decided that an imperfect area was done about as well as I was likely to build any time soon and left it alone.

In about a week of now-and-then progress, the depot was done. It's not a contest winner, but it certainly looks the part when placed into the crossing scene alongside a kitbashed interlocking tower and the brick Fable House hotel behind it.

Speaking of "fable," the moral to this story is that you can't know it all. If you have the data you need, you may not know precisely how to use it. If you can see a path forward for the

construction, you may lack the data. My advice is to press on, as you may never have all the information you need or develop the requisite skills needed to do contest-quality modeling.

A good example of going with what you have is Jack Burgess's model of the Yosemite Valley Railroad depot at Merced, Calif., **9**. It's actually the second model Jack built, as a previous effort was found dimensionally inaccurate after he acquired more information. For the same reason, Jack recalls that he built not one or two but three oil houses; see Chapter 8. (There can be pain associated with continuing a quest for more information.)

Nothing was really lost, as he gained modeling experience with each iteration and probably improved his techniques too. And Jack simply enjoys building models. His work is now regarded as of museum quality.

Don't reinvent the wheel

Modelers are notorious for coming up with a new way of doing something when existing methodology is working just fine, thank you. This is especially true when it comes to waybill systems controlling freight-car movements (see Chapter 8), but it applies to other matters as well.

To some extent, this is under-standable, as modelers are by nature a creative lot. But it's often a case of not doing one's due diligence, of failing to discover that a perfectly workable solution to a given problem already exists.

The first recommendation is to look to the prototype for inspiration—that is, don't reinvent the wheel.

Similarly, it's sometimes appropriate to follow the leader, but you may soon, or eventually, discover the leader didn't know where he was going. As long as the leader was doing something reasonably useful, that's usually not a problem. But it can cost time and money to backtrack to a new starting point. For example, as we'll discuss in Chapter 4, trying to save money by skimping on the underpinnings of our railroads, especially subroadbed, can create enough woes to relegate the railroad to abandoned-in-place status.

12

Book-ending our ambitions

Starting out with a clean sheet of paper is both like looking at unlimited potential and also intimidating. How can we get there from here? That leads to analysis paralysis: trying to gather everything we could possibly need to know about a whole host of options before cutting any wood.

We do have some up-front choices to make. Choosing wisely will indeed save time and money. But not choosing to do something now will cost even more time and money.

Among the decisions we need to seriously contemplate before making a choice is selecting an era to model. The more narrowly you define an era, the fewer purchases you will be tempted to make.

NKP Mikado expert Ray Breyer detailed a number of USRA light Mikados, both brass and plastic, for my NKP roster. All Brass Backshop's Mark Guiffre detailed other Mikes and added sound and paint, and Ken Dasaro weathered them. Detecting each 2-8-2's brass or plastic origin is now virtually impossible, and I saved considerable time by outsourcing this work.

How do you pick an era, often defined as a year or two? This is often one of the easiest decisions to make, but it can also be the hardest.

I may not be the person you should be listening to. When I built the freelanced Allegheny Midland starting in 1973, my goal was to model the late-steam era. But I quickly discovered that the brass locomotives I had that fit into my scheme of things—an Appalachian coal hauler with close ties to the Nickel Plate Road—were not only far too few in number but also not good performers or very accurate models.

The solution was to move the era up into the 1960s, thus allowing me to use some of the best commercially available models, including second-generation diesels, **10**. Since I was editing *Railroad Model Craftsman* at the time, it seemed wise to keep up with events on the full-size railroads, as my goal was to ensure that RMC tied modeling to full-size railroading. So the era marched steadily onward into the early 1980s when I left RMC for Bell Labs.

About that time, Key produced several excellent models of desired prototypes (most of which are still in service on my Nickel Plate layout).

So the era worked its way back to the steam age. In 1957, the NKP still ran steam on its southeastern Ohio coal lines and acquired EMD SD9s and Alco RSD-12s. Bingo—1957 was the ideal year to model, and I did that until the railroad came down around the turn of the century to make room for a new venture, the NKP's St. Louis Division, along which I had lived in the 1950s. The AM had lasted a quarter of a century, so it was "fully amortized."

Choosing an era to model for the NKP was even easier. I wanted to run steam—mainly Berkshires and

When master modeler Andrew Dodge decided to model the fabled Colorado Midland in O fine-scale (Proto:48), he discovered that no suitable steam models were available. So he scratchbuilt the needed fleet while maintaining the pace on the layout itself (*see Model Railroad Planning* 2015). *Two photos, Andrew Dodge*

Mikados—as well as Alco PA-1s on the two passenger trains, **11**. But Alco RS-3s, near the top of my favorite-diesel list, were delivered in April 1954. Steam came off the St. Louis Division in July 1955. So it made sense to model the fall of 1954, with steam in charge of handling the fall grain rush.

This book-ended my model purchases to models of prototypes manufactured before 1954 but not retired by 1954. For example, the popular Pullman-Standard PS-2 covered hopper debuted in 1955, so you won't find any on my roster.

It's worth spending a little time to make a chart showing a span of, say, ten years on the horizontal axis and a list of key events on your chosen prototype (or base prototype if you're freelancing) along the vertical axis. By "key events," I mean when favorite locomotives or rolling stock was acquired or retired, a new paint scheme debuted, passenger trains or symbol

freights debuted or were discontinued, cabooses were retired, running boards became passé, a depot or interlocking tower was demolished, a key industry closed (or discontinued rail service) or opened for business, a new signaling system such as automatic-block or CTC was installed, and so on. The chart will save time and money in the long run.

Model availability

When choosing a railroad, even a division of a railroad, and a year to model, consider model availability. If a model that meets your needs with regards to price, accuracy, and performance is not available, can you kitbash or scatchbuild the needed model? This will slow progress on the railroad itself; is that an acceptable trade? If not, can you afford to outsource the modeling chores, **12**?

When Andrew Dodge decided to replace his outstanding On3 depiction

of the fabled Denver, South Park & Pacific with an equally authentic ¼" scale model of the nearby Colorado Midland, he upped the ante by choosing to model in Proto:48, or O fine-scale. He described his efforts in *Model Railroad Planning* 2013 and 2015.

Andrew quickly discovered that 1:48 CM motive power was not available, so he couldn't do the relatively simple task of slightly narrowing the gauge and reshaping the wheel treads and flanges. Instead, he scratchbuilt brass models of a dozen or so locomotives, **13**. It slowed his progress on the railroad somewhat, but within a year of starting construction, the railroad was fully operational, as he explained in *Model Railroad Planning* 2015.

Note that Andrew had few if any options. Unlike my Allegheny Midland, the CM never made it to the diesel era, so he couldn't run the railroad with internal-combustion

Michael George built a multi-deck O fine-scale (Proto:48) model of a Louisville & Nashville branch. At least one class of locomotive used on the branch, a USRA light Mike, was imported by Overland, which offered a fine-scale wheel-conversion kit. Using the kit saved time for other projects, but modeling in P:48 to Mike's high standards is not a shortcut to finishing a layout. *Michael George*

power while he built up his steam fleet. Had I made a similar choice, I would still be learning how to fabricate the tender of the first engine with no place to run it. The lesson is obvious: Make hard choices based on your skill sets or risk getting bogged down from the outset. Scratchbuilding locomotives has a long tradition in the hobby, but it often becomes a time-consuming hobby in itself.

If he had chosen to model, say, a Union Pacific or Pennsylvania branch, odds are good he could have found models that could be converted to P:48. For example, Michael George obtained an Overland USRA light Mikado along with a kit to convert the model to P:48 specs, **14**, thus saving time he could spend on his multi-deck Louisville & Nashville layout (see

MRP 2019) and other models.

Model availability in any scale and gauge is therefore one of the very first steps in choosing what to model.

And remember what you deem good enough today may fall short of your minimum standards a few years down the line. If so, will you be able to purchase, kitbash, or scratchbuild the needed equipment, or will the inability to do so throw a wet blanket on the entire project?

Familiarity with the base prototype

You can save a lot of time by modeling something you're at least somewhat familiar with. Odds are, you'll choose a prototype or a base prototype (or two) if you're freelancing because you know something about it.

But you may have received a train set as a gift and found the paint scheme on the locomotive interesting. Those who received a Lionel or American Flyer train set for Christmas that happened to have an F3 or PA-1 painted in Santa Fe's incomparable red warbonnet scheme know exactly what I mean.

Owning a Santa Fe diesel and knowing anything about the railroad are two very different things. The good news is that learning enough about a specific railroad to do justice to it as a model is akin to embarking on an exciting expedition without the added adventure of being attacked by snakes, sharks, or man-eating mosquitoes.

Research can be the most rewarding and enjoyable aspects of building a model railroad. But it takes time, as we'll discuss in Chapter 2.

CHAPTER TWO

What to do ahead of time

Prior to starting your next model railroad, there are a number of important tasks you can initiate or complete, chores that you won't have time to address once construction commences. These may involve planning or be hands-on modeling projects. The latter assumes that you have made some hard-nosed choices about what to model, decisions that are among the greatest time-savers of all.

If your layout will occupy space that will also be used by the family, it needs to be attractive as furniture or in an artistic sense. In MRP 2015, Dennis Daniels described how he literally raised the roof on his house to accommodate a large HO railroad as well as an attractive family room. It's not hard to imagine getting more done on the railroad in such a pleasant environment. The use of power tools, however, should be restricted to the pre-evening hours. *Dennis Daniels*

I used Legato 22" x 23" carpet tiles by Milliken purchased at Home Depot. They come with interlocking serrated front and rear edges and are fully padded. They are also removable, making it easy to dry them if they get wet or to replace them if they are damaged by wear or hot solder or paint spills. Crews appreciate the padded tiles, and the layout room's appearance is greatly enhanced.

Layout room preparation

You can't make much progress on your next model railroad unless you have a place to build it. Ideally, that space should be inviting, comfortable, close to the family, and heated and air-conditioned or at least dehumidified. As we discussed in Chapter 1, you are highly unlikely to come home from a busy day at work and head out into a dusty garage, up into a boiling-hot attic, or down into a cold, humid basement.

Getting room preparation tasks out of the way up front while you're still engaged in layout research and planning avoids having this slow down the more fun aspects of building a model railroad. If these room enhancements improve the livability of the space, it's win-win: You get a better place to work, the family may gain more living space, 1, and the house is better situated for future resale. The cost of such renovations is therefore a legitimate line item on the general household budget.

Room improvements can be a handyman's job (as if you don't have enough on your to-do list already). But you'll save time and often get a more professional job by outsourcing the carpentry and electrical work. Moreover, the builder, electrician, or plumber may have some suggestions that will considerably enhance the space—move the water heater over there, reroute the stairs, build cabinets under the benchwork, add a branch electrical panel that controls all layout power and lighting circuits, and so on. They'll also avoid problems with building code violations. (We'll discuss lighting in Chapter 4.)

For the floor, I recommend thick rubber mats or padded carpet tiles that are not glued to the floor, 2. They are easier to fit into irregularly shaped aisles than regular carpet and can be picked up for cleaning or replacement if a water line bursts or you drop paint or hot solder on the floor.

A half-dozen or so of my tiles are drying as I write this, the result of ice clogging drainage channels in our backyard followed by a sudden rise in temperature and the attendant melting.

Roy Ward re-lettered a fleet of Atlas Geeps that were factory painted in the unique-yet-familiar Texas & Pacific livery for his Appalachian-based West Virginia Central & Pittsburg. He gently removed the factory lettering by rubbing it with a pencil eraser.
Two photos: Roy Ward

3

The melt-water ponded against the rear foundation, and a puddle formed in a small area of the basement floor. (I am already having French drains and a water-diverting stone wall installed.)

Locomotive selection

Freelancing, especially when basing your efforts on a specific prototype or two, will never go out of style. But this can be a huge drain on your meager allotment of hobby time. There are some shortcuts you can take that will save time, money, and effort while contributing to a more prototypical if mythical railroad.

As you chose a railroad to model, there are several ways to save time. One is to model a popular and usually large railroad that is well represented by commercially available models that are affordable, accurate, and excellent performers. You can shift your target slightly to do what's called prototype-based freelancing, or proto-freelancing for short. This entails using commercial models and slightly modifying them— perhaps only re-lettering them—to match your own needs.

One obvious caveat: I wouldn't try to adopt the Santa Fe's world-famous red-and silver warbonnet scheme for an eastern coal hauler or New York Central's gray pin-striped suit for a Northwest lumber railroad. It's better to follow in Roy Ward's footsteps by adapting a lesser-known scheme such as the one used on Texas & Pacific's

Geeps, **3**. It exhibits many of EMD's standard painting cues for hood units but for most modelers isn't in-your-face familiar.

The Tennessee RR retained the Rutland yellow-trimmed-green paint scheme when they acquired some ex-Rutland Alco RS-1s. I followed their example when my freelanced Ridgeley & Midland County, which interchanged with the Allegheny Midland at South Fork, W.Va., also acquired former Rutland RS-1s. I patched over the Rutland lettering and applied custom R&MC decals, **4**.

I was more creative when I painted and lettered a pair of Alco Models RSD-12s in a paint scheme that combined elements of the Nickel Plate

Good example: The Rutland's green-and-yellow Alco-designed scheme migrated south to the Tennessee Railroad, and then to my Ridgeley & Midland County short line, thanks to Atlas factory-painted Alco RS-1s and custom road-name decals.

Bad example: Being too creative can be a liability. I combined elements of the NKP and Rutland paint schemes when painting a pair of Alco Models RSD-12s. The result was a pleasing and plausible paint scheme, but it would have been quicker and easier—and the AM's ties to parent NKP even more obvious—if I had used commercial NKP stripe decals.

Road's post-1959 scheme with the Rutland paint scheme, **5**. This required masking the stripes, and it failed the final exam, which was to create a paint scheme that clearly evoked the AM's parent railroad, the Nickel Plate. I then bought diesels already painted in NKP livery and simply re-lettered them, or I used NKP decal sets to add the striping to black-painted shells, **6**. Much easier, much more plausible.

This applies to freight cars too. It's much easier to buy a factory-painted model for the base prototype and simply change the road name and reporting marks with custom decals, **7**.

Many railroads used locomotives designed by the United States Railroad Administration (USRA) during World War I, **8**. These were handsome machines and have been offered in most scales. Of course, over time each railroad made modifications either to the originals or post-war copies, notably distinctive headlight styles, longer tenders, modified cabs, and so on. Find a railroad that had appealing USRA locomotives and plagiarize.

Other examples: Six Union Pacific 4-6-6-4 Challengers were leased to the Rio Grande during WWII. They found homes on the Clinchfield as 670–675 in 1947, joining Alco war babies 650–663. So when UP 4-6-6-4 3985 headed east in 1992 and temporarily assumed CRR livery as 676 (the number following the last CRR number), **9**, it was an authentic re-creation of history, and a UP Challenger in Appalachia barely stretches the fabric of plausibility.

Steam authority Karen Parker cites another example of Western power finding a home in the East: Central of Georgia (as well as Western Pacific) got copies of Southern Pacific's Gs-2 4-8-4s during WWII. It doesn't quite justify lettering an SP Gs-4 like 4449 in Central Appalachian livery, but it comes close.

Some of the Norfolk & Western's 10 home-built, rough-riding K3 4-8-2s were sold to the Richmond, Fredericksburg & Potomac, and the remainder went west to the Rio Grande before they were all acquired by the Wheeling & Lake Erie and, following the Nickel Plate's lease of the

6 I striped this Atlas RSD-4 using Herald King EMD Geep decals. (More recently, Microscale produced striping designed for Alco hood units.) Better still, Atlas produced their RS-3 in NKP livery, which would have made the job even easier.

7 Removing the factory-applied road name and reporting marks and replacing them with custom decals is much quicker than painting and lettering a car, as is evident on this pair of AM and NKP triple hoppers. I custom-painted and -lettered this brass NJ International caboose, but today I would simply re-letter an Atlas plastic model already painted in the NKP's High Speed Service scheme.

The USRA family of steam locomotives was an especially handsome lot. Examples of almost all USRA wheel arrangements—such as this light 2-8-2 Mikado detailed for still-extant NKP Mike 587 when it still had a short tender, and a 2-8-2 lettered for Frank Hodina's proto-freelanced Chicago & Illinois Western (obviously part of the Chicago & Illinois Midland family)—are available in most scales, often at attractive prices, making them excellent choices for a freelanced steam roster. Details such as headlights, number boards, extended cabs, feedwater heaters, and larger tenders can give your fleet a family appearance.
C&IW photo: Bob Hanmer

Wheeling in 1949, by the Nickel Plate Road. (Sunset imported HO models, **10**, one of which saw service on the Allegheny Midland.) So there are some examples of Eastern designs heading west and vice versa. But, like my caveat about too-well-known regional diesel paint schemes, discretion is advised.

Other than the USRA line of locomotives, some designs were shared among several railroads because of common ownership or by restrictions in new designs during World War II. The Advisory Mechanical Committee coordinated locomotive designs on the Chesapeake & Ohio, Erie, Nickel Plate Road, and Pere Marquette, which resulted in very similar 2-8-4 Berkshires, especially on the C&O (where they were called Kanawhas, usually pronounced "ka-NAWS"), NKP, and PM. The Richmond,

Fredericksburg & Potomac also bought engines of this same basic design, **11**. The basic "Nickel Plate Berk" has been produced in every popular scale, so it can serve as a good freelancing base for railroads east of the Mississippi.

But a Pennsylvania K4s Pacific or New York Central J-3 Hudson would look wildly out of place in the Pacific Northwest or Southwest, just as a Santa Fe or Southern Pacific Daylight 4-8-4 would look more than odd traversing Horse Shoe Curve or steaming along the Hudson except in modern-day excursion service. So choose your battles carefully.

The safest approach for freelancers is to choose an unremarkable locomotive and then detail or at least paint and letter it to resemble other engines in your fleet. The prototype modeler may similarly get by with a not-so-accurate

model by adding details that make it look more at home.

But the constraints fall away for those modeling short lines, as more often than not they employed second-hand motive power, **12**.

A plausible diesel roster

Those modeling the diesel era have it much easier. It's hard to name a diesel that hasn't been offered in HO and in several other scales as well. But, as with the plain-vanilla USRA locomotives, railroads tended to customize their fleets to some degree, **13**.

Which brings us to diesel paint schemes. Those modeling first-generation diesels have their hands tied to a degree in that the builders—notably Alco, Baldwin, Electro-Motive Division of General Motors (EMD), and Fairbanks-Morse—had their own

Near duplicates of Union Pacific's highly successful 4-6-6-4 Challengers were built for the Clinchfield, an example of a Western design that successfully migrated into the Appalachians. On November 11, 1992, CRR "676" negotiates terrain that, despite the Armour Yellow support cars behind it, looks nothing like the Challenger's usual stomping grounds. *Ron Flanary*

Among Norfolk & Western's least-successful designs were the K3 Mountains, which were palmed off on the Rio Grande and the Richmond, Fredericksburg & Potomac before being reunited on the Wheeling & Lake Erie. A few of these rough-riding beasts made it onto the Nickel Plate Road roster, which happily passed them on to my Midland Road subsidiary.

11

The talented Advisory Mechanical Committee formed by the Van Sweringen-owned railroads created the powerful Lima-built 2-10-4 for the Chesapeake & Ohio. It was slide-ruled down 75-percent to create the highly successful 2-8-4 Berkshires used by the C&O (where they were called Kanawhas), Nickel Plate, Pere Marquette, and, in cosmetically altered form, the war babies for the Richmond, Fredericksburg & Potomac shown here. *Courtesy C&O Historical Society Collection (c&ohs.org)*

12

The famous Strasburg Railroad in southeastern Pennsylvania uses former Great Western 2-10-0 no. 90 and ex-Norfolk & Western 4-8-0 no. 475 to haul both tourists and freight. Both are unusual prototypes, but they look like cousins as employed on the Strasburg, setting an example for giving a family appearance to the steam roster of a freelanced short line. *Rich Taylor*

styling departments or contracted that out to noted designers. Even the most cursory review of EMD F units and "Geeps" will show that the styling department reused the same design themes time and time again, **14**. So freelanced paint schemes in the transition era and well into the 1960s should follow typical locomotive builders' styling conventions.

If that sounds restrictive, think of it this way: By copying elements of a prototype scheme, you're almost assured that your freelanced models will look plausible. You may also discover that you can mask off a section of the model and change a color to create a new look, **15**. Or you can at least use the prototype scheme for inspiration.

I recently chatted with Eric Brooman, well known for his outstanding Utah Belt HO railroad. The paint schemes he has applied to his diesel roster over the decades as he strives to keep the railroad up to date are not copies of any prototype scheme, but they look the part, **16**.

I asked him about whether he considered prototype-based freelancing more time consuming than prototype modeling. "The freedom afforded by

13

Even "plain vanilla" hood units can be detailed to achieve a family appearance, as was the case on Brian Moore's HO Southern Pacific layout in the U.K. "Tiger-stripe" SD7 5330 displays the SP's as-delivered configuration with a "barrel" or "ash-can" Mars signal light at either end. SD7 1509 has the 1979 upgrading with full front-and-rear signal light packages. Both are Proto 2000 models to which Details West lights, sunshades, and other parts were added. (More recent releases have these details factory-applied.) No. 1509 was repainted after the under-slung tank was removed. *Two photos: Brian Moore*

14

The relationship between the Erie Lackawanna (bottom) and Algoma Central (top) paint schemes is obvious. This practice allows freelancers to adapt a prototype scheme with new road name decals and perhaps some detail changes without unduly assaulting the plausibility barrier. EMD styling studio designers often reused graphic elements such as stripes but changed the colors.

15 Mike Confalone's freelanced Allagash Railroad set in Maine (top) has gone through several iterations of diesel paint schemes because of era shifts. His Alco RS-36s wear a green-and-yellow livery that stylistically borrows heavily from one of neighboring Delaware & Hudson's later paint schemes (bottom). *Prototype photo: Jeff Martin; model photo: Mike Confalone*

16 Eric Brooman has kept his freelanced Utah Belt up to date for several decades. His background as an art teacher has helped him to capture the look and feel of Western railroading to a remarkable degree. But having to create custom decals and to paint and letter every piece of UB rolling stock takes more time than using factory-painted and detailed models.
Eric Brooman

17

Before I started construction on the Allegheny Midland, I assessed what custom decals I would need and drew the needed artwork 8 times larger than HO scale. Even less-than-perfect artwork often looks good when significantly reduced, but watch for thin lines on serif typefaces that disappear and narrow openings that fill in. Many railroad typefaces are now available online.

freelancing, in my opinion, outweighs any extra work involved with painting and decaling," he replied. "Besides, that is one of the aspects of modeling that I really enjoy.

"By freelancing, I mean prototype-based freelancing," he added. "There is a huge difference, as you have pointed out many times. I avoided a lot of the difficulties that were mentioned by John Armstrong by setting the UB in an area devoid of railroads.

"When I was modeling the Southern Pacific," Eric recalled, "the frustration of trying to compress reality into the basement of a bi-level house proved too much for me. As anyone who has traveled to the area that I pretend to be modeling can attest, it looks nothing like my layout. The whole thing is a controlled fantasy. I just couldn't do that to Donner Pass."

Custom decals

If at all possible, prepare the artwork for and order custom decals prior to starting layout construction. Once the saws and drills come out, it may be years before you again have time to do artwork or paint and letter models.

This often applies as much to prototype modelers as well as freelancers in that commercial decals

of the desired color, size, and accuracy may not be available. The Nickel Plate Road Historical & Technical Society's Modeling Committee is continuously assessing the need for custom decals despite the tendency of today's modelers to prefer factory-painted models—which admittedly are great time-savers.

Preparing artwork for a sheet of custom decals need not be onerous. There are many railroad-theme type-faces available online, and even hand-drawing master art doesn't have to be as neat as you might imagine. If you draw it eight times larger than the needed size, when it's reduced to scale size by the decal printer, your art may be perfectly fine, **17**. The main concern is that thin lines don't disappear or open areas fill in when reduced to scale size. Use a photocopier to check.

Just as proofreading text is always a good idea, be sure to have a friend check the spelling of any prepared artwork. A good friend assumed that the famous Moffat Road was not absorbed by the Rio Grande. When I had a chance to admire his railroad, I noticed his sizable diesel fleet was lettered MOFFIT ROAD in rather large type. I assumed this was to honor a friend with the different spelling but,

being a nosy magazine editor, I asked him about it.

He gave me a blank stare, grabbed *The Moffat Road* hardcover book off a library shelf, looked at the cover—and swore. We both learned a hard lesson that afternoon, and when I later did my own decal-sheet art, I triple-checked everything.

Base prototypes

We've discussed using standardized locomotive designs and paint schemes on freelanced railroads, but plausibility —if that's a concern—goes much deeper than that. It's a good idea to follow a base prototype to save time and effort on all aspects of your modeling endeavors.

Layout-design guru John Armstrong (1-1), whose freelanced O scale railroad was called the Canandaigua Southern, once said that plausible freelancing was much harder (hence time-consuming) than prototype modeling. His reasoning is that the prototype modeler has well-defined benchmarks to measure his or her efforts against. For the prototype modeler, a careful study of the chosen prototype, which is often supported by a railroad-specific historical society, will take you well along the road to modeling success.

Unlike parent Nickel Plate Road, the Midland Road was set in the central Appalachians. The AM therefore followed NKP painting and lettering guidelines but employed six-motor Alcos and EMDs and copies of some Chesapeake & Ohio steam such as this 2-6-6-2, an upgraded Pacific Fast Mail import. Depots and other lineside structures were also based on C&O prototypes.

Ted Pamperin models the Chesapeake & Ohio during WWII. His roster needs were well supported by commercial models: From left to right, a T-1 2-10-4 from Broadway Ltd., an H-4 2-6-6-2 from Bachmann, an H-8 2-6-6-6 from Rivarossi, an L-1 streamlined 4-6-4 from Broadway Ltd., a C-16 0-8-0 (under the sand dock) from Lambert, and on the turntable a J-3a 4-8-4 from Broadway Ltd. Only the Lambert switcher is a brass import that required work to bring it up to today's expectations. *Ted Pamperin*

Bill Darnaby adapted Hallmark's Illinois Central 4-8-2s to look more at home in Ohio by changing the tender and sand dome and adding a Worthington feedwater heater and pumps, plus a Standard stoker. Note how a larger Delta trailing truck from an AHM heavy Mikado helps to fill in the space under the firebox. Similar changes could be made to plastic locomotives to achieve a family look or to more closely resemble another prototype. *Two photos: Bill Darnaby*

The freelancer, on the other hand, has to do the same homework on the base railroad (and there may be more than one base railroad: AM = NKP + C&O), and then extrapolate that information to create a similar but different faux prototype. I can think of quite a few well-known modelers who have pulled this off successfully, but I don't think any would say they saved time and effort by taking that approach.

Moreover, prototype modeling is so much easier today than it was a decade or two ago. When I started to convert the Allegheny Midland back to the steam–diesel transition era in the early 1980s, good (in terms of both appearance and performance) brass models were just starting to be available in a decent variety of prototypes. I had a pair of Pacific Fast Mail C&O H-6 2-6-6-2s from the 1960s, **18**, that were at best coffee grinders with minimal pulling power. It took the expensive talents of gifted model builder Joe Borick of Cheat River Engineering to make them usable. Key then came out with similar 2-6-6-2s of USRA design that needed very little improvement.

Today, Bachmann makes less-expensive DCC- and sound-equipped models of the same locomotives.

This aids the freelancer and prototype modeler alike. The C&O steam modeler, for example, **19**, can choose from a good variety of relatively inexpensive, ready-to-run (well, almost) steam locomotives. The time and money spent adding extra details and weathering is much less than rebuilding an early brass locomotive.

Another approach to achieving specific roster objectives without scratchbuilding a fleet of locomotives is Bill Darnaby's fleet of Maumee Route 4-8-2 Mountains, **20**. Bill's original goal was to model the Monon ("MOE-non," not "mon-un") in the diesel era, but he realized that diesels allowed the Monon to run longer, hence fewer, trains, which would greatly reduce the dispatching challenges on a model railroad. He also found that modeling the steam era on the Monon was not supported by manufacturers or importers back then.

He therefore created the carefully conceived Cleveland, Indianapolis,

Cincinnati & St. Louis—the Maumee Route—with new and used Hallmark Models imports of the Illinois Central Mountains as the mainstay of the CIC&StL fleet. After he acquired three new Mountains, he discovered they often weren't expensive on the used-locomotive market, as they had a flaw in the gearbox design. But Bill, a mechanical engineer, knew how to remedy that. He also wanted larger tenders, which were borrowed from AHM/Rivarossi NKP Berkshires.

"The IC did not believe in appliances," Bill notes, "which resulted in plain-looking engines. I added Worthington SA feedwater heaters with the coldwater pump under the cab, which fills a huge empty space behind the firebox and prompted a larger (AHM) trailing truck. A Standard stoker engine helped in that regard too. I also replaced IC's distinctive angular domes with large Kemtron castings." The result is a distinctive yet highly plausible fleet of locomotives, most acquired at a reasonable cost and without having to scratchbuild major components.

Even so, Bill has often noted that if he were starting from scratch today, he'd model the pre-diesel, single-track Chicago, Indianapolis & Louisville (Monon) in 1947. He has acquired the needed imported Overland 4-6-2 and 2-8-2 steam locomotives, which weren't available when he launched the Maumee. Cast-resin kits for Monon passenger cars are also available now, saving construction time.

In any event, the time to gather and detail a fleet of locomotives, cabooses, and passenger and freight cars is before you get busy building the railroad. If you discover, as Bill and I did, that the available locomotives weren't quite up to the tasks they needed to perform, you can adjust your plans or even choose a different part of your favorite prototype, or even a different prototype, to model.

(We found that his ex-IC 4-8-2s and my NKP 2-8-4s would not pull the 20- to 30-car freights we had envisioned in the uphill direction of our multi-deck, continuous-spiral railroads. Panic ensued! Fortunately,

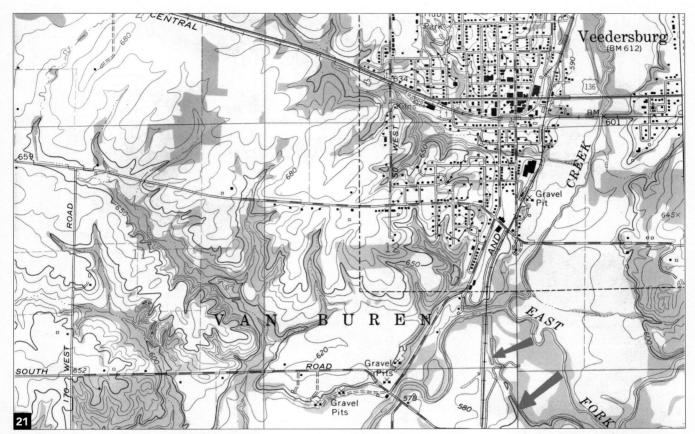

21 U.S. Geological Survey "quadrangle" topographic maps provide considerable information about land contours, the general layout of towns and industries, and roads and railroad grades (including abandoned lines). This section of the map showing Veedersburg, Ind., shows the Nickel Plate (here running north–south) crossing the Peoria & Eastern. The arrows show where geometric shapes of contour and tree lines give clues to the location of the abandoned Chicago, Attica & Southern alignment.
U.S. Geological Survey

Bill started his railroad a decade or so before I began mine, and he had discovered that using metal wheels such as those produced by InterMountain and NorthWest Short Line greatly improved an older car's rolling characteristics. With every car so equipped, steam's performance crept forward to an acceptable level.)

Car and train movements

Another important pre-construction step you can take is to get the paperwork out of the way. It's good to have settled on how you plan to orchestrate car and train movements ahead of time. You can then get a head start on finding samples of prototype paperwork such as rulebooks, timetables, dispatcher train sheets, train orders, and waybills.

We're very fortunate to live in a time where there are railroad-specific historical and technical societies that typically have massive collections of exactly the paper forms we need. There are often organizational subject-matter experts who understand how the full-size railroads operate(d) and can help you gain insights into what your chosen segment of a railroad did for a living and how it did it in various eras.

Better still, gaining access to these experts and the needed files is much easier than in the pre-internet days. The key: Get as much of this homework done before you find yourself busy with benchwork and wiring.

Research shortcuts

Speaking of homework, there's nothing like a lack of information to stall a project. Wondering how a town or industry was actually arranged is a good example. The most basic sources of such information are U.S. Geological Survey quadrangle topographic maps, **21**. Sanborn fire-insurance maps, **22**, are also very helpful and are typically available through historical societies and large state universities or libraries. Railroad-specific historical societies may have copies of the U.S. governments valuation maps produced during WWI, **23**. These to-scale drawings and the associated field notes and photos are available at the National Archives Annex in College Park, Md. Pens and pencils aren't allowed, but cameras and scanners are welcome.

Aerial photos can be extremely helpful. For example, check the listings on Jack Burgess's and Chris Ellis's websites, respectively:

• www.yosemitevalleyrr.com/clinics/prototype-research-reference-list-july-18-2011.pdf (scroll down to the maps section in the "clinics" section of Jack's site)

• adenarailroad.blogspot.com/2014/12/how-to-use-usgs-earthexplorer-website.html?m=1

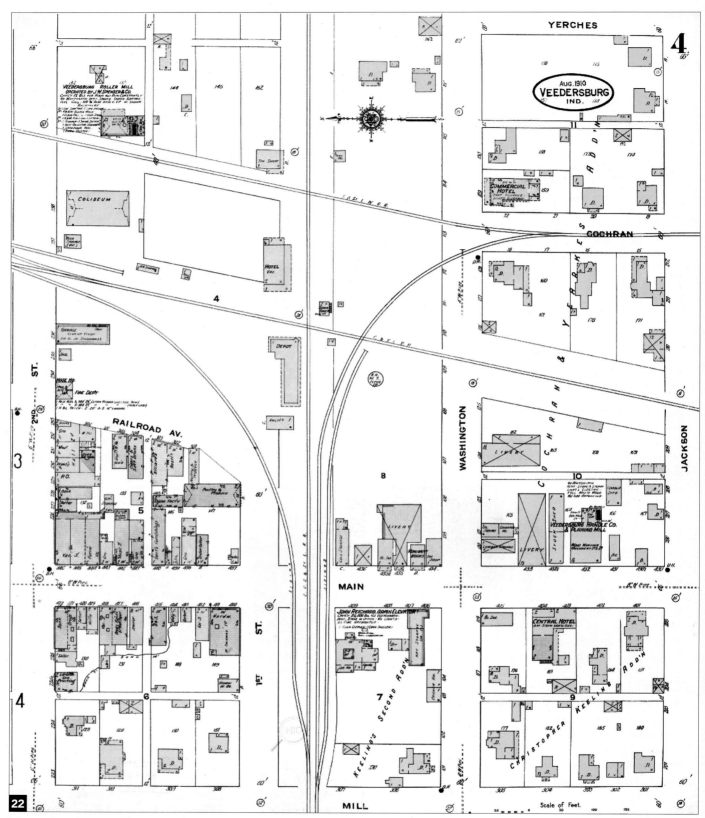

Many state university libraries and some historical societies have color or black-and-white copies of Sanborn fire-insurance maps. They provide detailed information about structures and approximations of railroad alignments. This August 1910 map shows downtown Veedersburg, Ind., with north to the left, where the parallel Toledo, St. Louis & Western (later NKP) and Chicago & Eastern Illinois (later Chicago, Attica & Southern, abandoned following World War II) crossed the CCC&StL (Big Four, later Peoria & Eastern). The NKP and part of the P&E depots still stand; all three railroads have been abandoned.

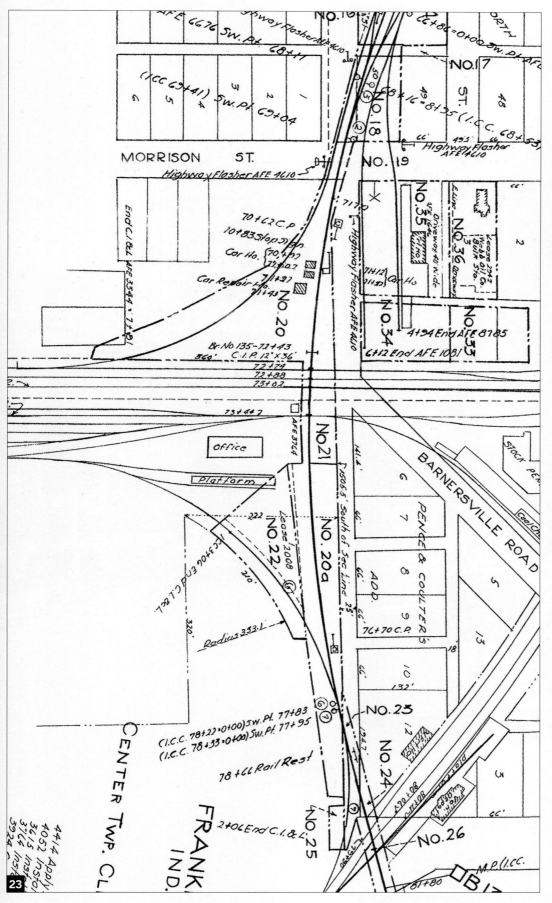

Valuation maps—this section of one shows the NKP-Monon and Monon-PRR (Vandalia) crossings in Frankfort, Ind.—were prepared for the government when it took over U.S. railroads during World War I. They were often updated for decades after the railroads resumed control and are a gold mine of information about track arrangements and structures. The originals are in the National Archives Annex in College Park, Md.

1 Mike Burgett's HO Chesapeake & Ohio James River line depends on units such as this EMD F7 from Athearn Genesis passing M Cabin at Major, Va. Most of his motive power is factory painted, Mike reports. "The recent flood of accurate C&O diesels has been great. Most of us quickly discover that we have time to lavish on building a railroad or painting equipment, but not both at the same time. Getting the railroad running should be our first priority." *Craig Wilson*

CHAPTER THREE

Looking to the prototype

Building a model railroad requires employing a wide variety of skills and knowledge, although some of the work—even layout construction, as we'll discuss in Chapter 4—can be outsourced. Modelers often push ahead without doing enough due diligence about full-size railroading, and often as not that leads them down blind alleys. Looking to the prototype, **1**, can save time, money, and frustration.

Layout Design Elements

For those who are modeling a specific part of an actual railroad, the choices of what to model are confined to a limited (hence time-saving) but appealing set of choices, **2**. And the obvious approach to designing a layout is simply to find track maps and other information (often through railroad-specific historical societies) about terminals and towns that, strung together linearly and in geographical order, would together comprise an interesting model railroad. This is especially helpful for the neophyte, as his or her track-design skills are minimal; plagiarizing actual locations is almost sure to provide more pleasing and plausible results.

Beginning in the inaugural (1995) issue of *Model Railroad Planning,* an annual issue of *Model Railroader,* I coined a convenient label— Layout Design Elements, or LDEs—for visually and operationally recognizable models of actual locations such as towns, yards, engine terminals, waterfronts, memorable scenes, **3**, industrial complexes, and so on. The basic idea is that we can choose the best candidates from among many found along a division of a given railroad, string them end-to-end in geographical order connected by segments of main line, and be reasonably certain that the resulting track plan will look and operate like its prototype.

My entire railroad, based on the Nickel

Randy Laframboise and Mike Sparks have done a remarkable job of replicating in miniature scenes and structures from Vermont's Rutland Railroad in the transition era. Their HO model of the Sheffield Farms creamery at Ferrisburg, Vt., is an example of the balance between saving time by not having to search for good modeling candidates (as the freelancer has to do) and spending the time needed to build an accurate model. *Model photo: Randy Laframboise; prototype photo: Laframboise collection*

Plate Road's St. Louis line between Frankfort, Ind., and Charleston, Ill., is nothing more than a series of LDEs connected by segments of rural main line, **4**. Had my space been more limited, I could have chosen a few busy towns and connected them together with mainline segments and with staging at both ends. Even a single-town layout fed by staging on either or both ends would be well worth the effort. If yard switching was my favorite pastime, I could have modeled only the Frankfort, Ind., or Charleston, Ill., yard, again fed by staging at both ends.

The two images of Linden, Ind., **4**, clearly make the point. I made the sketch for my Kalmbach book about LDEs, *Realistic Model Railroad Building Blocks* (2005), long before the scenery was relatively complete. Yet the differences between the imagined and modeled scene are paper-thin.

That's because the sketch was made using prototype track diagrams, maps, photographs, and data gleaned during field trips, and the model was based on the sketch. In short, I did my best to plagiarize using information about an actual place in a narrowly defined time frame (early 1950s).

How this saves time

Knowing a great deal about where you are heading makes it a lot easier to get there from here. This is an advantage that the prototype modeler has always had over the freelancer who also strives to produce a plausible, authentic-looking model railroad.

Those who base their freelancing efforts on one or a few related railroads can gain most of the advantages the prototype modeler has at his or her disposal simply by following the same path: Find interesting (from both a visual and operational standpoint)

locations to model, study them enough to determine what's important and what can be discarded, and make a to-scale sketch of various ways to capture the key features in a reasonable area.

After you have made sketches of several potential Layout Design Elements, arrange them—preferably in geographical order—on a same-scale drawing of your layout space. It's much like solving a puzzle and can be very entertaining. You'll probably find that not everything fits, and that you may have to discard one or more locations. You may need to go back to the drawing board as you search for a more compact substitute.

In a surprisingly short time, you will discover that you have designed your next model railroad as far as major town and scene locations are concerned. Don't forget to include a place for staging at one (stub-ended

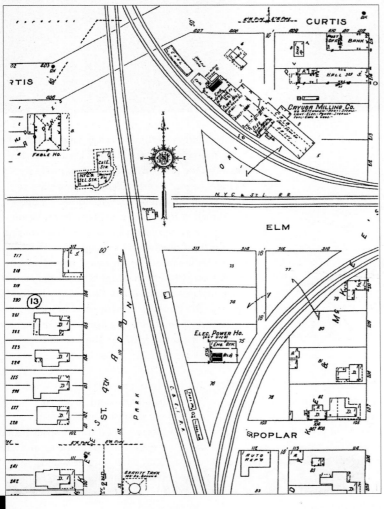

3

I modeled a favorite scene I clearly recalled from my hometown—Cayuga, Ind.—in the 1950s: the wood interlocking tower guarding the Nickel Plate–Chicago & Eastern Illinois crossing, the joint depot, and the Fable House hotel. The tower was an easy kitbash using a Walthers plastic kit (6-2), the depot is scratchbuilt (1-8), and the hotel uses walls made from photos I shot and backdated using Photoshop Elements that were glued to a styrene core, 6-14, the latter a relatively quick way to scratchbuild structures. At left, a Sanborn fire-insurance map from 1913 shows the same structures and illustrates why these maps are excellent reference tools.

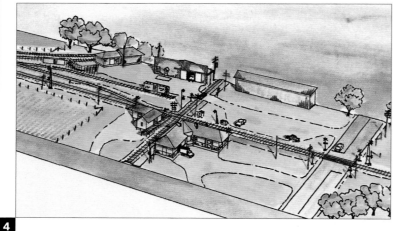

The NKP crossed the Monon at Linden, Ind. The busy interchange there (12,000 loads swapped between the two railroads in 1953) made it an ideal Layout Design Element candidate to model from an operational standpoint. I drew the sketch at left using prototype information years prior to modeling the scene. The crossing was north of downtown, so only a few buildings had to be modeled, which saved time. Frank Hodina scratchbuilt the depot; I built the freight house using a kit issued by the Monon Historical Society. The house is a stock Atlas model repainted white, which is a good "default" color to use to keep the focus on the railroad.

branch or short line) or both (through route) ends. Then it's simply a matter of connecting the LDEs with segments of main line.

Hint: Put the relatively featureless mainline segments on narrow shelves; 8" to 12" should suffice. This saves time and money while gaining aisle width, as we'll discuss in Chapter 4.

Pitfalls of using prototype info

Much as I advocate doing a lot of homework about your chosen prototype (or base prototype for freelancers), and as enjoyable as discovering needed information can be, there is real danger in becoming bogged down by analysis paralysis. As I'll repeat often within the covers

of this book, you will never know everything you want to know.

As we discuss Layout Design Elements, we're taking a rather broad view of each candidate location. Later on, we can worry about whether we have enough information to build a good model of this depot or that lumberyard. For now, let's focus on the

Brian Moore used a "stock" Tichy water crane on his Southern Pacific layout until he could locate a key part: the large wheel that turns the valve on and off. It's a small model but is a very distinctive "signature" addition to an Espee steam-era layout.
Three photos: Brian Moore

Big Picture—the general appearance of the location, what tracks we need to model and why, how much space we need to allow for key structures (perhaps they can be represented by flats or even photographs on the backdrop to save space—and time and money; see Chapter 6), any problematic scenic features such as an upper-deck water course that intrudes into the "air rights" of the lower deck (Chapter 5), and so on.

At some point, we have to "kill all the engineers" and actually start building something. This will often be at an uncomfortable point in the development of the railroad where you know you need more information, and you also know that you aren't getting any younger or anything done on the railroad.

You have three choices: Do more homework; build what you can with the information you have but avoid projects where information is lacking; or build stand-ins that look the part but should eventually be replaced. (Fair warning: Stand-ins have a way of growing deep roots.)

British modeler Brian Moore offers an example of a good-enough stand-in that was replaced when a needed part became available:

"I used an as-constructed Tichy kit for the water column at Guadalupe, Calif., on the Southern Pacific, which I model in HO (2-13 and 6-5). It looked great and is in a prominent position. Most people wouldn't notice that the

water column lacked the prototype's large hand-wheel control. Meanwhile, it served its intended function.

"I was finally able to replace the stand-in with a more accurate version," 5. "It took me many months of searching for something similar-looking to that wheel," Brian recalls. "A fellow modeler here in the U.K. finally found a 1/43-scale wheel of the correct size in his spares box and sent it to me.

"I then built another Tichy kit and modified it accordingly with that fabulous wheel," he reports. "It's a might thick, but the Guadalupe water column is finally accurate."

Like Brian, when a needed model can't be created now, I don't advocate leaving a bare spot on the railroad if a stand-in is readily available. Filling the space with a reasonable for-now model looks better and helps to convince the layout builder and viewers alike that progress is being made. And, when you're done with the stand-ins, you can "pass them forward" to another modeler to help him or her have a better-looking railroad more quickly.

The most important aspect of layout construction, many of us have found, is to get the main line installed and operating between staging yards, even if it goes through future yards and town sites with nary a turnout installed. Having an operating railroad draws other modelers, and many of them will offer helpful ideas or constructive criticism.

But beware of too much specific

advice, such as "You need to install a crossover right here." If your prototype didn't deem one necessary, you probably won't either. You'll usually save time by following the blueprint and ignoring "helpful" advice.

An example is the engine terminal in the Nickel Plate's yard at Frankfort, Ind. A locomotive needing to leave the engine terminal and reach the head end of a westbound train has to negotiate a labyrinth of switchbacks and crossovers to get across the main line between the east- and westbound yards. A crossover at a key location, 6, would have made the move a lot easier. There had to be a good reason to omit it that is probably lost to time, but in any event I am not going to install one despite several comments to the contrary. This saved the time and money required to modify two Shinohara no. 8 turnouts to "DCC-friendly" status.

One track diagram of the NKP in Metcalf, Ill., shows not one but two crossovers; a later one shows no crossover. It's a small town with a single NKP-switched industry, a grain elevator, so I figured I didn't need either crossover. Mistake. What I overlooked was the Baltimore & Ohio interchange, which—unlike the elevator that shipped primarily to the east—offered cars headed both east and west. Including a crossover, 7, would have created a short runaround, making it much easier for westbound through freights to retrieve the westbound cars.

I could retrofit a crossover, but that

NKP road locomotives heading to the westbound yard at Frankfort, Ind., had to negotiate a series of switchbacks that could have been minimized with an additional crossover where marked in green. But the NKP didn't add that crossover, so I didn't either.

I wrongly assumed that a crossover near the depot at Metcalf, Ill., was an extravagance I could ignore, only to discover that including one would have greatly eased the task of picking up eastbound cars from the Baltimore & Ohio interchange. Adding a crossover now would entail a lot of work, as part of the siding would have to be raised a scale foot to mainline height.

is a Very Big Deal at this stage. Both turnouts that comprise a crossover have to be ballasted to the elevation of the main line. The siding then slopes away from both ends of the sidetrack turnout down to the level of the un-ballasted (except for a bed of cinders) siding. So

I'd be tearing up several feet of track to correct my mistake.

This error should have been caught during initial operating sessions long before ballast and other scenery invaded the scene. But I rarely serve as a road crew, and no one who did

mentioned this to me. They probably figured that, like Frankfort, that's just how things were arranged.

A similar problem exists at Veedersburg, Ind., **8**, but here I can again blame the Nickel Plate. There was a crossover exactly where one is needed to facilitate westbound pickups, but it disappeared in the 1940s. About the same time, a crossover mysteriously appeared near the much busier Monon interchange in Linden, Ind. My guess is that the need at Linden was much greater than at Veedersburg, so it was moved. Why not leave the Veedersburg crossover in place and install a new one at Linden? Maybe Shinohara was temporarily out of code 70 no. 8 turnouts …

Another good example of the value of using the Layout Design Element approach is the track arrangement at my 1950s hometown, Cayuga, Ind. The NKP switched a Standard Oil dealer, a lumberyard via a team track, and my dad's brickyard, and they also got loads from a grain elevator and the Chicago & Eastern Illinois interchange. There was also a long passing track at

8

To pick up westbound cars at Veedersburg, Ind., the Nickel Plate's westbound local (oddly, there was no eastbound local on the Third Subdivision) has to pull them off the interchange or team track and run east to the end of the passing track to get around them and shove them onto its train. A crossover (red) would have made this easy—and in fact one was there until the late 1940s!

Cayuga. But there were several extra tracks, notably the North Track and the Storage Track, **9**, whose purpose I didn't understand. By following the LDE methodology—plagiarize!—I dutifully installed them. Thank goodness!

Cayuga was conveniently located at about the midpoint of the run between the Frankfort and Charleston terminals. We soon discovered that adding all of the empty boxcars needed for soybean loading along that subdivision usually exceeded the capabilities of the USRA light Mikados that typically handled No. 45, the westbound local. What to do?

Why not stick half of those empties in a through or extra freight and tote them west to, say, those storage tracks at Cayuga? There the KC Local could "reload" with empty boxcars for the second half of its daily trek to Charleston. That's what those tracks were for, and they were just sitting there waiting for us amateur railroaders to figure it out!

So there are two major pitfalls

9

The Nickel Plate interchanged with the Chicago & Eastern Illinois at Cayuga, Ind. Almost any type and quantity of freight cars could be delivered to or picked up from the C&EI on this track, but the adjacent track serving Thompson's grain elevator loaded only a few cars a day. Interchanges are therefore a key reason to model railroads with lots of them.

to watch out for: Doing too much homework without getting started on the railroad, and indiscriminately eliminating things that you have yet to figure out.

Applying our knowledge

Now that we've chatted about what to do and what not to do, in Chapter 4 we'll explore some timesaving ways to apply them in three dimensions.

1

CHAPTER FOUR

Shortcuts to layout construction

A good way to save time, especially if you prefer to build models rather than benchwork and even scenery, is to outsource layout construction. Lance Mindheim (shelflayouts.com) notes that customers typically want him to build a layout that's mechanically and electrically complete, including track with ballast. They can then concentrate on scenery and structures. *Lance Mindheim*

If caution is warranted in any aspect of layout design and construction, it is during the latter. Like building the foundation of your home, it's hard to fix the underpinnings after the railroad is well along. Overbuilding is a much better approach than skimping on benchwork and especially subroadbed. Nonetheless, there are ways to save both time and money without building in a sizable amount of regret, as we'll explore here as well as in Chapter 8. And layout construction can be outsourced, **1**.

For the HO Port of Los Angeles, Bernie Kempinski used an open-grid frame made from 1 x 2 pine with 2" pink foam for the flat terrain. He found some dips in the foam and in the future plans to use a layer of ¼" plywood on top of the foam to provide a flatter surface.
All: Bernie Kempinski

2

The Big Picture

"You can fill an entire gymnasium with benchwork in a long weekend." Before we get into the nuts and bolts of layout design and construction, this quote by the late Jim Boyd needs to be memorized. Better yet, type it into your computer, print it out in large, boldface type, and tape it to the door of your railroad room.

Fear of taking the first giant step—that is, moving from ideas and research to actual construction—can be very intimidating. Given the tiniest foothold, such fears can delay progress for years.

There's no need for that. With a few basic tools—tape measure, saber saw, power drill, level, and maybe a table or circular saw (most large-scale cutting can be done for you at a lumberyard or

big-box store), you're in the benchwork business. An inexpensive laser level (or rent one to set benchmarks around the room) will make it easier to ensure everything is measured precisely from a constant elevation.

Outsourcing some parts of layout construction to a professional adds to cost but gains a huge savings in time. You can choose where the pro's work begins and ends: benchwork, benchwork with track and wiring, full scenery, help with structures, and so on.

One experienced professional, Lance Mindheim (shelflayouts.com), notes that "The current project in my shop [1] is typical of the job scope I see the most often. It's a proto-freelanced Detroit, Toledo & Ironton HO layout set in the 1960s in the Detroit–Flatrock, Mich., area with an emphasis

on the steel industry. Dimensions are roughly 12 x 20 feet.

"Most customers want a layout that's mechanically complete without scenery and structures. As is the case here, many also have me paint and ballast the rail and at least rough in the scenery contours so all they have to do is add textures and vegetation. This job is controlled with NCE DCC wireless plus Tortoise switch machines and Tam Valley frog juicers."

We've already discussed how to reduce the track planning chores to the equivalent of assembling a picture puzzle, one where you supply the pieces called Layout Design Elements. (See **3-4** and my book, *Realistic Model Railroad Building Blocks,* Kalmbach, 2005). Given a track plan, or at least a good mental picture of where you're

47

Most of the 16"-wide upper deck of my NKP layout is supported every 16" by inexpensive stamped metal brackets fastened to wall studs. This required notching the backdrop panels, which made installation around lower-deck curves time-consuming because I had already installed the roadbed. The drooping blue "cable" is a rope light that works well to simulate a moonlit night.

starting, where you're going, and what you want to encounter along the way, you can move to the benchwork phase immediately.

This is also a good time to take a brief look at how master modeler Bernie Kempinski built his HO depiction of the Port of Los Angeles using IKEA's IVAR bookshelves as the supporting structure. This not only saved time and effort but also provided an attractive furniture look to the railroad, which is in one corner of his TV room.

The railroad, **2**, was has an open-grid frame made using 1 x 2 pine and 2" pink foam for terrain. "This layout depicts a very flat area that was built on fill," Bernie points out, "so no hills were needed. But the pink foam did have some dips and areas of uneven thickness. In the future, I will bond a layer of ¼" plywood on top of the foam so the track will be on a flatter surface."

He adds that he likes to use pocket screws for open-grid benchwork and cuts the cross pieces with a miter saw for precise right-angle cuts. The fascia

is a piece of ⅛" hardboard.

Bernie stained the IVAR uprights a dark blue but did not stain the shelves. "I have found that books and magazines sometimes stick to shelves with stain or polyester or polyurethane finishes," he cautioned.

A logical sequence

It will save time to tackle layout construction tasks in a logical sequence. The one I'm suggesting here was developed after I encountered problems with the backdrop installation step.

Assuming you have a good idea where the benchwork goes, step 1 is—remembering Jim Boyd's "gymnasium" comment—to build the benchwork.

If you follow my example of making a full-size drawing of the railroad on kraft paper (or printing a CAD drawing out full size), as I describe in the next section, step 2 is to put the paper template atop the benchwork as a final check of sightlines and reach-in obstacles and distances.

Step 3 is to install the backdrop. On my multi-deck NKP layout, I found

this difficult to do on the lower deck after the subroadbed and roadbed were in place. I had to cut an 8-foot long piece of hardboard into two 4-ft. lengths where it curved around the end of the peninsula. I couldn't just slide the longer piece into place, as the top edge had notches that fit around the L-shaped shelf brackets every 16", **3**. This created another seam between backdrop panels that can be prone to cracking. Had the track structure on risers not been in place, the task would have been much easier.

Speaking of hardboard backdrops, if you use this material, it pays to seal both sides before installation. Interior latex paint won't seal them; ask your paint store for a product like marine varnish that will.

Step 4 is to install the lighting if it is situated over the layout behind valances. If you're using ceiling fixtures to cover wide areas of the layout, lighting installation would be step 1.

Step 5 is to install subroadbed on risers, roadbed, and track.

Step 6 is to do the wiring and test-

4

Photos dating to the early 1970s show the template I drew on kraft-paper on the floor from my ¾"-scale Allegheny Midland track plan; the first 1 x 4 benchwork; the long kraft-paper template partially unrolled on the benchwork; an optimistic me checking a tunnel portal position; and a view of the peninsula showing the standard 40" benchwork height. Track elevations ranged from 43" to 58", but I kept the benchwork top surface at 40" to allow the paper templates to be unrolled atop the benchwork as a final check on track positioning, reach-in distances, viewing angles, and other features.

5

Allen McClelland used Homasote splines for an extension to the original Virginian & Ohio and throughout the second V&O. They ensure smooth easements into curves and dead-quiet operation, establish a ballast profile, and combine subroadbed and roadbed construction. *Paul Dolkos*

run the railroad. For a multi-deck railroad, remember to plan wire routing paths from the upper deck behind the backdrop to the main bus wires under the lower deck. For DCC, ask your DCC supplier whether the bus wire pair should be loosely twisted. Even with DCC, break the railroad into manageable-size blocks, each with its own booster, to make troubleshooting easier. Basic operating sessions should commence to find design errors and to encourage progress on all fronts.

Step 7 is to add the valance, fascia, and landform scenery. You'll be amazed at how finished a model railroad looks sans scenery but with the backdrop, fascia, and valance in place.

From paper to plywood

When I designed the Allegheny Midland back in 1973, I first made a ¾"-scale drawing. When that looked good, I laid rolls of kraft paper on the basement floor and transferred the small-scale drawing to a full-

size template, **4**. When that looked reasonably good and aisle width was deemed sufficient, I used that template to cut the benchwork, which was conventional-grid (essentially boxes of 1 x 4 lumber). It was still too early to begin to cut the subroadbed from ¾" plywood.

With the benchwork erected to a constant 40" height, I unrolled the kraft paper atop the framework and checked reach-in distances. In key areas, I inserted sheets of heavy cardboard or plywood under the kraft paper and placed models of trains and structures to make a final check of accessibility.

With everything looking good, I then cut out the roadbed from ½" Homasote, which was considerably cheaper than plywood in case I made a

6

Jeff Otto's entire railroad, yards and all, rests atop Homasote splines. He is a fastidious modeler and has a professional railroad background, so his handlaid track is constructed to very high standards. An overview of his iron-ore-hauling railroad was the *Model Railroad Planning* 2013 cover story. *Jeff Otto*

David Barrow has long advocated building model railroads large or small from 2 x 4-foot "dominoes" that ensure a linear approach to layout construction and accommodate changes easily by simply cleaning off or changing the top surface. No room for a layout? Build a domino! Dominoes can be arranged into almost any shape, and as the finished scene shows, once the scenery is added, viewers don't know what kind of benchwork lurks below.

David Barrow

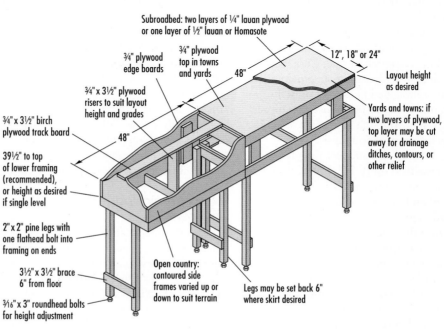

Subroadbed: two layers of ¼" lauan plywood or one layer of ½" lauan or Homasote

¾" plywood top in towns and yards

¾" plywood edge boards

12", 18" or 24"

48"

Layout height as desired

¾" x 3½" plywood risers to suit layout height and grades

Yards and towns: if two layers of plywood, top layer may be cut away for drainage ditches, contours, or other relief

¾" x 3½" birch plywood track board

48"

39½" to top of lower framing (recommended), or height as desired if single level

2" x 2" pine legs with one flathead bolt into framing on ends

Open country: contoured side frames varied up or down to suit terrain

3½" x 3½" brace 6" from floor

Legs may be set back 6" where skirt desired

³⁄₁₆" x 3" roundhead bolts for height adjustment

7

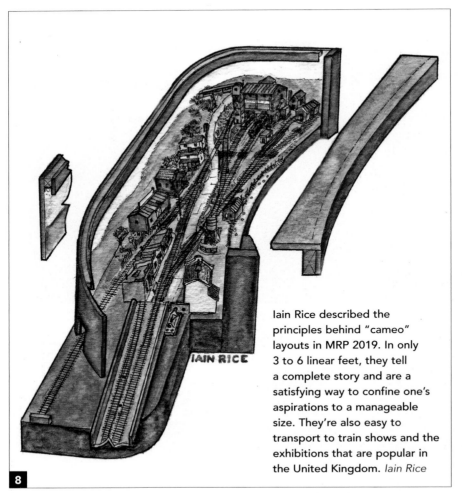

Iain Rice described the principles behind "cameo" layouts in MRP 2019. In only 3 to 6 linear feet, they tell a complete story and are a satisfying way to confine one's aspirations to a manageable size. They're also easy to transport to train shows and the exhibitions that are popular in the United Kingdom. *Iain Rice*

8

mistake. I then used the Homasote as a template to cut the plywood, offsetting the joints between lengths of plywood and Homasote by at least a foot.

I keep hearing that modelers are using ½" plywood for subroadbed. I don't recommend that: I use ¾". Remember my earlier statement about the subroadbed being not only the "foundation of your house" but also extremely difficult to replace or shore up if thin plywood sags?

I would also support the plywood subroadbed every 16". I once stretched this quite a few inches in a staging yard and discovered that over time it had sagged enough to require shims under the track. That was easy to do in an unballasted staging yard but would have been a pain to deal with on the scenicked portion of the railroad.

I have never used spline roadbed, but I can attest that Allen McClelland's roadbed made of vertical Homasote splines was the quietest

roadbed I have ever (not) heard. And it saves a construction step in that the splines comprise the subroadbed and roadbed in one package, **5**. Allen told me it went up very quickly once he got the hang of it. Jeff Otto has also used Homasote splines on his sprawling iron-ore hauler (see *Model Railroad Planning* 2013) and is delighted with the results, **6**.

My only caveat is that when you're cutting Homasote, be sure to do it in a neighbor's garage. Or try using a metal-cutting or knife-edge blade.

Narrow-mindedness as an asset

There's nothing that saves more time than erecting a sheet of plywood on a pair of sawhorses and slapping down a loop of Snap Track. But plopping a large surface into the middle of the room (you will need access on all four sides of a 4 x 8) wastes a lot of space. So we'll confine our discussion to

layouts with vastly more potential and much less inconvenience.

When it comes to building a realistic model railroad, linear track plans are infinitely more flexible and a quite easy to build. So cutting that 4 x 8 sheet into two 24" x 96", three 16" x 96", or even four 12" x 96" pieces is a much better idea.

David Barrow has often written about his aptly named "domino" approach whereby you construct a standard-size, light frame, add a top plate made of plywood, and nail down some track, **7**. You can build dominoes at your workbench or another convenient working surface where back strain is unlikely to intervene. If you tire of the track arrangement or have changed modeling themes or improved your scenery skills, simply peel off the top plate and start anew, something David is also famous for doing.

There are also modular standards such as Ntrak and Free-mo. The latter are especially useful in that you retain a tremendous amount of flexibility in the track design. (See "Modeling the Linden St. freight station" in MRP 2019.)

So even if you have a tightly defined track plan for the Atlantic & Pacific RR, you may lack the space, experience, or funds to dive into the deep end of the pool right now. Building a portable, sectional, or modular (interchangeable sections) layout may be the better alternative.

Those of you who live in a college dorm or an apartment may be overlooking a golden opportunity to build at least a portion of a future layout—an LDE, perhaps. We all need bookcases, and their top surfaces just beg to be the base of small model railroads or segments of larger ones.

A more refined version of a small layout called a cameo, **8**, was described in detail by famed British modeler and layout designer Iain Rice in MRP 2019. Cameos were designed for the busy United Kingdom exhibition circuit, but they are equally suitable for home layouts or North American train shows and conventions. By limiting the scope of the project, they also save considerable time, effort, and funding.

9

A pair of PFM C&O 2-6-6-2s were poor performers and needed details, paint, and weathering. Joe Borick of Cheat River Engineering did a masterful job of doubling the pulling power, and Dennis Regan painted and weathered them. The money spent saved me a huge amount of time that was better spent on the railroad.

Without being asked, good friends Frank Hodina and Randy Laframboise volunteered to build, respectively, the L-shaped NKP-Monon depot for Linden, Ind. (3-4), and the V-shaped NKP-B&O depot for Metcalf, Ill. (above). This not only saved me time but also serves as a most pleasurable reminder of the importance of building not only railroads but also friendships among hobbyists. The grain bins are resin castings available from Frank's Resin Car Works.

I enjoy handlaying turnouts, but where diamond crossings are concerned, not so much. Trackmeister Jim Lincoln was therefore commissioned to build the many diamonds that mark sites where foreign railroads crossed the NKP and provided lots of interchange traffic. In the flatlands, that was about every ten miles.

Mark Guiffre of All Brass Back Shop improved the suspension and installed sound decoders in these factory-painted Overland imports, NKP Alco RS-3s 543 and 546, and associate Ken Dasaro did his usual masterly weathering job. After painting and lettering dozens of locomotives for the Allegheny Midland, I'm happy to farm out these tasks today, thus saving time that is better spent on the railroad. Moreover, adding nose stripes to a brass hood unit's grab irons can be a major undertaking.

Several experienced modelers will have more to say about this approach in Chapter 8.

Outsourcing time-consuming tasks

Most of us take considerable pride in our modeling accomplishments and enjoy sharing our work with visitors and our operating crews. On occasion, I even invite my wife to critique my work, although I have learned she is a tough critic and doesn't cut me any slack just because we happened to be married. We also enjoy various aspects of model building and layout construction more than others.

It might be nice to be able to divide the various projects we need to complete before our model railroad is ready for prime time into those we enjoy doing and those we don't, and then to outsource all of the less-pleasant tasks.

Perhaps a more practical approach is to divide them into those we have time to do and those that are holding up progress, and then outsource the roadblocks, even if down deep we know we'd take a great deal of satisfaction in doing them ourselves.

Painting and lettering a Chicago & Eastern Illinois E or F unit or, worse, a BL2 is not an easy task, but Phil Monat did so not once but twice, one for a friend in Indiana and one for me. When he's not busy painting engines or managing theater lighting designs on Broadway, he's also one of my yardmasters.

When I built the Allegheny Midland with very little outside help—no regular work sessions, for example—I handlaid the track, scratchbuilt the turnouts, painted and lettered AM locomotives and rolling stock, installed what we then called "receivers" (DCC decoders today), and so on.

I was younger then and apparently had endless drive and energy. I also needed to buy a lot of hardware for the railroad, so disposable income was spent on that rather than on outsourcing work.

But as the railroad developed, I found that there were some tasks

14

Perry Squier realized that using SPDT micro slide switches could both move the switch points and change the frog polarity. He then wired up a hundred or more slide switches at one time rather than doing a few at a time as needed, thus saving time in the long run. He hides the knob under an NJ International switch stand and instructs crews to moves the knob with an uncoupling skewer.

that were repetitive, and others were above my comfort level in terms of having the needed tools and/or skill sets. This was especially true when it came time to get the brass steam fleet tuned up (or, especially in the case of articulateds with poor front-engine drive mechanisms, rebuilt), painted, and weathered, **9**. By that time, I had more disposable income, so the process

of outsourcing difficult tasks (but never layout construction and scenery work) became an important aspect of sustaining progress on the railroad.

I discovered that having a pro help me with some tasks did not diminish my enjoyment of the railroad nor my feeling of accomplishment when it reached the operational stage and finally became fully scenicked.

When I dismantled the AM around 2000 to provide space for a new railroad, I was mentally well equipped to deal with decisions regarding what I could and would do myself and what I would outsource. I didn't keep careful records, but I believe the time from starting construction on the AM to driving the gold spike was about a decade, whereas on the NKP that time was cut roughly in half despite the fact that the NKP is multi-deck, which is the equivalent of building two or more railroads in the same footprint. Clearly, I had learned some hard-won lessons.

For the most part, and with the exception of a staging yard, I glued down all the track myself, ballasted every inch of it, did all the scenery, and so on. But when two expert modeling friends—Frank Hodina and Randy Laframboise—volunteered to build the depots at Linden, Ind., and Metcalf, Ill., **10**, I was only too happy to have their support and proud to have their work represented on my railroad. Jim Lincoln built the multiple diamond crossings where foreign railroads cross the Nickel Plate, **11**.

Speaking of diamond crossings, to save time I initially ran the NKP main through the diamond-to-be sites without regard for the future diamonds, as the crossings contribute nothing to operations. The unpowered dummy foreign-road tracks, which typically

15

Another project railroad built for an MR series to be published in 2020, this one in O scale, is based on a small Hoosier town on the Nickel Plate's St. Louis line. It was also built on 2" foam board and employs folding-leg tables in lieu of wood benchwork. It could be built as one or two sections and expanded as space permits.

extend only 16" to 24" between fascia and backdrop, were simply butted up to the NKP stock rails.

Mark Guiffre (All Brass Backshop) and Frank Feko have handled my locomotive "enhancement" needs and decoder installations, and Mark's associate Ken Dasaro weathers most of my steam and diesel fleet, **12**. And my regular Frankfort westbound yardmaster, Phil Monat, custompainted a C&EI BL2, **13**.

I even outsourced the track planning to Frank Hodina when my own efforts, which were tied too closely to how the AM had fit into our basement, came up short. At first, I was a bit uncomfortable not being able to design my own railroad, but Frank was able to use the Layout Design Element approach (I chose the towns) without his hands being tied by preconceptions.

The final plan is a relatively simple design that runs around the perimeter of the basement as well as long both sides of a long central peninsula (see December 2014 MR). Frank strung the LDEs together in geographical order, and he also made three hugely important design contributions by commandeering the back 9 feet of our garage, locating the main yard along the longest wall, and providing a yardmaster's alcove between the yard and perimeter wall at the other yard.

There were many others who have made and are making important contributions to the railroad. But it's still my railroad, and none of these most-helpful contributions have in any way diminished my pride of ownership and accomplishment. And they saved me a lot of time and false starts.

So, just as "plagiarism is our most important product," outsourcing to friends or professionals can also be a key factor in getting a railroad built and operating with fewer missteps.

Peer pressure

You're going to tire of me repeating this mantra, but I'll say it again here: Bring your railroad to an operational stage as quickly as possible and operate regularly, as crews will expect to see and also appreciate progress.

I'm not suggesting that you

16

Inexpensive stamped-metal shelf brackets are adequate to support benchwork up to perhaps 16″ deep. Beyond that, I use the stronger, longer snap-in double-slotted shelf brackets available at big-box stores. The benchwork here is 24″ deep. The slot spacing requires the use of shims to match elevation changes on grades.

need to dive headfirst into realistic operation with a dispatcher, operator(s), timetable, CTC system, waybills, and other features. I *am* saying from long experience that anything you can do to attract fellow modelers to regularly visit your railroad to see what you've gotten done will greatly abet progress. You'll be excited to show them something new (or fixed), and they'll be interested in seeing your latest accomplishments. They know, and you know, that excuses—even those firmly grounded in truth—about not having enough time or being worn out from the daily grind sound a bit hollow month after month.

Layout construction

You've read my case for using visually and operationally recognizable models of actual locations (Layout Design Elements) to ease track-planning chores. Now let's explore some ways to save time and maybe money as we begin to convert paper or digital plans into 3-D reality.

And remember that LDEs can be used as the basis for layout sections or interchangeable modules if space for

the dream layout remains elusive. You can feed each LDE with a portable (maybe on casters) staging yard on one or both ends. If more space becomes available, build another LDE and move one staging yard back a ways to accommodate it.

We've discussed commercial layout designers and builders. There are also suppliers of pre-fab benchwork components that you assemble. Samples I've seen are of very high quality.

Building things in multiple can save time. This is one of those "Do-as-I-say, not do-as-I-do" situations. It's better you follow the example of Perry Squier, who lives just down the street from me and (as you will see in Chapter 6) is a superb model builder.

To wit, Perry is a master at ganging up repetitive tasks and projects. When "we" needed to wire a zillion SPDT micro slide switches to move our switch points and change the polarity of our frogs, **14**, Perry sat down at his workbench, cut the needed quantity of all of three colors of wire for the leads, and soldered the whole shebang at once. I, on the other hand, would have cut enough wire for maybe a dozen switches, and done that repeatedly as needed.

"Portable" layouts

Let's discuss "portable" layouts that don't have to be portable. In the August through November 2005 issues of *Model Railroader*, I described how I built the F-shaped 1:29 Claremont & Concord using slabs of 2" foam that rested atop standard 30"-wide folding-leg tables, **1-4**. This negated the need for benchwork. The layout was in four 30" by 8-foot sections that, with the structures removed, were relatively light. And the tables could be found at almost any hotel or convention center, saving transporting them to shows.

More recently, I built a one-town O scale railroad for a series in MR scheduled for 2020. I employed the same foam base and tables, **1-5** and **15**. I transported it to the O Scale National near Washington, D.C., in the back of a small SUV.

But let's consider another possible use not involving shows. Let's say that you live in an apartment and know you won't be there for years and years, and you don't want to attach anything to the walls or damage the flooring. Buy a few folding-leg tables and some foam board, and you have the makings of a model railroad that can easily be moved when the need arises.

Or let's say you now have a permanent home layout, but like me you're not as young as you used to be. Concerns about who will be tasked with dismantling and removing the railroad when you move to a retirement community have been bothering you. And then there's the chore of restoring the room to a living space for the next owner.

Consider putting a "best if used by" date on the railroad and hiring a contractor or bribing some friends to remove it well ahead of any retirement relocations. Then you can … sit on your hands with no model railroad. Or not. You could buy some folding-leg tables and sheets of foam board and build a railroad that will be easy to remove when the time comes.

17

Permanent home layouts

More optimistically, let's assume you're about to build your next permanent home layout. It doesn't have to be as big a chore as we've often considered it to be in the past.

If you follow my example, which followed Bill Darnaby's example, and build a layout comprising narrow shelves, construction can be barebones simple and extremely fast. Whether single- or multi-deck, for the narrow shelf segments, you can simply screw shelf brackets into studs on 16" centers. For shelves less than 16" wide, I typically use L-shaped, stamped-metal brackets costing less than $2. For wider shelves, I used double-slot brackets that snap into vertical channels, **16**.

Atop that goes a layer of ¾" birch plywood. It costs more than cheap AC-grade plywood, but splurge and buy cabinet-grade birch plywood with as many plies as you can find. Resist the temptation to skimp on the foundation.

On top of the plywood, for the main line I usually add two layers of ¼"-thick milled Homasote from Cascade Rail Supply (cascaderailsupply. com). I use ¼" plus ⅛" milled roadbed for other tracks, as they're not ballasted but simply rest atop a layer of cinders (except on some Western railroads that had oil-fired steam locomotives). Milled roadbed goes down fast and saves making a mess while cutting sheet Homasote in your neighbor's garage. It's also uniform in thickness, whereas sheet Homasote tends to thin

I use ⅛" tempered hardboard for fascias and valances. I paint them using a "CTC machine green" olive color (also see photo 5-4). This color blends nicely with vegetation and murky water and avoids the need to carefully paint along the top edge of the fascia.

out across the narrow ends.

Homasote is a nearly ideal material when handlaying track, as it holds spikes nicely. But if you're using commercial track, there are several other types of commercial roadbed such as cork and foam.

The ½" height of mainline roadbed allows for ditches on either side, even in the Midwestern flatlands (which actually aren't very flat). To create the field side of the ditches, I fasten ⅜" foam sheets, available in 24" x 48" accordion-fold bundles at big-box stores, **5-13**. This raises adjacent fields and building lots enough to create a ditch but still leaves the main line standing tall. Using these foam sheets

allows this work to be finished in minutes, and the foam provides an ideal matrix to hold stems of small bushes, SuperTree trunks, and JTT corn stalks (**5-14**).

In wide areas where conventional benchwork is required such as yards, I used ¾" AC-grade plywood ripped into 1 x 4s. The plywood "lumber" is much straighter and probably less expensive than pine lumber.

You *can* make a project out of building benchwork: Don't. Just cut the outside framing and interior joists to length, lay them out in the desired pattern, coat the ends of one "stick" at a time with yellow (not white) carpenter's glue, and hold the two

pieces of plywood together as you run no. 8 x 1½" coarse-thread drywall screws through one and into the other. No pre-drilling or countersinking is required. Yes, you will occasionally split the end of the piece that abuts the outside frame, but the yellow glue will hold it in place.

An alternative to conventional-grid benchwork is L-girder, pioneered by former MR editor Linn Westcott. It is more flexible in that you can more easily achieve rounded corners and peninsula ends, but it can't be used on the upper decks of a multi-deck layout, where thinness is a primary virtue. By the time you add up the thickness of the track, roadbed, subroadbed, and

18 It's easy to curve Central Valley's nicely detailed turnout tie strips by cutting the spacing strips along one edge. (The ties supporting the frog and adjacent rails are not curved.) I was therefore able to use no. 8 turnouts in a ladder originally designed for straight no. 6 turnouts at Charleston, Ill.

19

lighting, you'll find that's as much thickness as you want to cope with while avoiding compromising the sightlines to the lower deck(s).

Fascias and valances

Back when I built the Allegheny Midland, faux wood paneling for fascias and valances was all the rage. Both were often angular. By the time I built the Coal Fork Extension, painted and smoothly flowing fascias and valances were in vogue, as they are today, **17**. This is triply good news, as wood paneling (faux or real) is more expensive than plain sheets of tempered hardboard, and the chosen style has an annoying habit of going out of production the week before you need another two 4 x 8 sheets. Moreover, it's hard to patch a wood-pattern fascia.

What color to paint the fascia and valance is a matter of taste, but most veteran layout builders agree that it should not stand out like a gilded picture frame. Those modeling the East, South, Midwest, and Pacific Northwest might opt for a dull green, whereas someone modeling the arid Southwest might prefer a tan.

I followed David Barrow's

suggestion in MRP 1995 to use a color close to that applied to Union Switch & Signal Centralized Traffic Control machines. I'll discuss other uses for this color in Chapter 5 on scenery.

2-D to 3-D

I mentioned my technique of drawing the track plan full size on the floor, then transferring that to a sheet of Homasote, which in turn became the template for cutting the more expensive plywood.

Once the track centerlines were drawn on the kraft paper, the paper was stapled to the Homasote. I then used an awl to poke holes through the centerlines into the Homasote every few inches. When I removed the staples and kraft paper, I simply connected the dots (indentations) with a medium-point felt-tip marker. I then measured ¾" off either side of the centerline and cut the Homasote roadbed using a saber saw along those lines.

With the roadbed cut out, I placed it atop the plywood making sure the Homasote and plywood butt joints were well offset, and that the plywood was used as efficiently as possible.

The plywood was then located atop the benchwork and elevated on risers to the desired elevation. Finally, the Homasote was yellow-glued to the plywood subroadbed.

I cut my ties from ³⁄₃₂"-square basswood. A typical railroad tie measures 7" high by 9" wide, the latter being close to ³⁄₃₂" in HO. This has two benefits: First, you don't have to worry about which side of the tie to insert in a tie-spacing jig (another time-saver when laying lots of track); and when you sand the top surface smooth, the resulting thickness will be close to a scale 7".

While watching television, thus (sort of) saving modeling time, I inserted ties into a 2-foot-long wood jig and held them together with ¼"-wide strips of tape. These were hung like machine-gun belts of ammunition along the benchwork. When a sizable quantity of tie strips was on hand, I applied a thin coat of yellow glue to the Homasote roadbed and laid down a strip of ties. They were centered on the roadbed by eye.

The ties were not stained prior to gluing them down. That's because they have to be sanded to a uniform

A commercial LED fixture intended for under-cabinet use produces a reddish (around 3200K) light. Moreover, when the LEDs are less than several feet above the track, as shown here, each LED head may create a distracting streak of light across the rails. In my experience, diffusers don't help much, so I suggest testing fixtures or strips of LEDs before buying them in quantity.

height, thus removing any stain, and the natural variations in the hardness of the basswood will create different densities of color anyway.

For the Nickel Plate, I handlaid several turnouts in one town. To meet a layout-tour open-house deadline, however, I installed Micro Engineering no. 6 turnouts off the main line and upgraded Shinohara no. 8s for all crossovers and mainline turnouts.

In the Charleston, Ill., yard, however, I used Central Valley no. 8 tie strips. By cutting the outer webs between ties (except near the frog), they can be curved, **18**. These ties are hollow, so they accept regular track spikes. The ties are also highly detailed with grain and tie plates. There is a flat area where a cast Details West frog can be attached with CA, making accurate frog location and rail gauging straight-forward.

With handlaid ties that are sanded, stained, and ballasted, I can cut and file the rail for the stock, closure, guard, point, and frog rails, spike everything down, and fill (with soft solder) and file out the frog in well under an hour. With CV ties, I glue the ties down with DAP clear adhesive caulk, paint

the ties a deep brown color with a spray can, then spike down the rails. Last comes ballasting.

Adding a little more time in both cases, feeder wires to the bus wires under the table are attached to the back (away from the aisle) side of the rails using silver-bearing solder.

If you're using flextrack, take a tip from veteran layout builder Chuck Hitchcock and glue it down using DAP clear adhesive caulk (use DAP: Accept no substitutes). I tried another brand and found the track wandered around—especially on superelevated curves—before the caulk fully set.

If you're using commercial turnouts, make photocopies of each type of turnout (templates may be available online), and use them as templates when laying out yard ladders and complex industrial tracks. Note that Micro Engineering now has HO codes 70 and 83 Track Ladder System turnouts that will save both time and space. Templates are available online at microengineering.com.

If you plan on handlaying track, FastTracks has a huge variety of templates that greatly ease the task of building turnouts and crossings. My

neighbor Ted Pamperin handlaid the turnouts for his first layout using those jigs and is delighted with the results.

Faced with the unwelcome time-consuming, tedious, and expensive task of installing more than 175 switch machines and associated wiring, Mike Sparks and Randy Laframboise decided to use PECO Insulfrog turnouts with over-center springs that hold the points to one side or the other. No additional wiring was needed. There is a dead spot on the frogs that can affect short-wheelbase engines, so they installed "keep-alive" circuits in every locomotive, which also improved performance elsewhere.

Randy reports that the use of hand-thrown switches creates a more intuitive and realistic operation than having to search for a button to push on the fascia. "The time and expense saved was enormous," he concluded.

Lighting the railroad

I built both of my home layouts before LED lighting was available. In both cases, I used cool-white fluorescent tubes, which are rated around 4100 Kelvins. I have some 5000K tubes purchased through an electrical supply

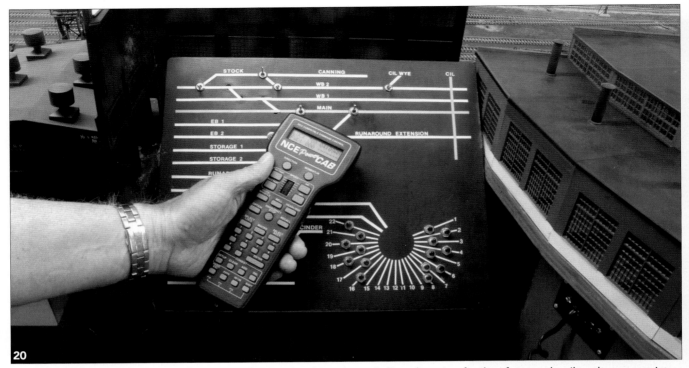

DCC wiring can be as easy as running a pair of bus wires along the main line, dropping feeders from each rail to the appropriate bus, hooking the bus wires to a plug-in panel, connecting power from a "wall wart" plug-in transformer into the back of the panel, and powering the railroad through an NCE PowerCab. The Power Cab can also be used as a regular plug-in throttle as shown here.

house, but I don't recommend them for several reasons: To my eye, they are a bit too harsh or cold, even though printers use them to check colors; they are expensive; they aren't available on Saturday evening when a key fixture fails; and they don't come in a wide variety of lengths and diameters. (An F8 tube is ⅝"–1"—in diameter, an F5 is ⅝", and so on.)

I deal with color all the time in my magazine and book work, so I am sensitive to color shifts. But I have placed models of various hues, especially reds and blues, under 4100 to 4300K light and could not detect a color shift. Note that this is not the same sort of test as having two identical models placed in adjoining cabinets illuminated by different-temperature lighting; there some subtle differences might be noticeable.

But we face all sorts of compromises when we deal with colors and lighting. Our layout lighting is a tiny fraction of the intensity of the sun. So what subjectively looks good is more than likely good enough. Don't waste time trying to come up with the perfect

lighting scheme unless you have professional expertise in that arena.

At this writing, LED lighting is becoming more popular as prices drop. I have some LED lighting on my layout, and it ranges from needs-to-be-replaced to very good. Many commercial fixtures produced light in the 3000K range, which is very red. But an even greater concern, at least to my eye, is when LED lighting "heads" are placed close to the rails, as is often the case on a multi-deck layout. In those cases, you can see a bright stripe of light across the shiny railhead every few inches—at the same spacing as the LEDs, **19**. As I walk along the main line, those stripes seem to sweep past like driving by the end of an Iowa cornfield and looking down the rows.

Replacement LED "tubes" for fluorescent lamps are available, and they seem to have better diffusers built into them than even some of the high-end LED lighting systems for, say, kitchens. Some require that you cut out the ballast inside the fluorescent fixture, which could be very time-consuming; others do not.

In any event, weigh your options carefully to avoid expensive and time-consuming missteps, as it's a whole new world where lighting is concerned. And be sure to read Bernie Kempinski's comments on layout lighting in Chapter 8.

Also be aware that there are electrical codes that govern the number of "devices" such as outlets and lighting fixtures on any line from a circuit breaker. Rather than doing your own 120VAC wiring, it may be safer and quicker to have an electrician install a series of outlets around the railroad room, perhaps on the ceiling, and plug lighting fixtures into them.

Layout wiring

Hooking two wires—one plus, one minus—from a direct-current (DC) power pack to the rails has been a part of scale model railroading since the beginning. If you have an oval of track, or even a linear switching layout operated by a single locomotive, that still works pretty well.

It's when you start to move closer to typical railroad operations that

DC begins to get complicated. If you plan to have two operators run two locomotives at the same time, you need a toggle or rotary switch to connect each block to Cab A or Cab B. That also requires twice as much block wiring. Three engineers running three locomotives? Triple the wiring. Having the headlights on and at a constant brightness takes some special equipment, and realistic sound is much more limited.

The bottom line here is that using Digital Command Control (DCC) is more electronically complicated but much easier to use. And almost all of the complicated part is done for you by the manufacturers who make DCC control systems and decoders. It's like using a computer for basic chores such as email, Web searches, and writing simple documents: You don't have to know how it works to enjoy using it.

DCC wiring is very simple: Run a pair of bus wires around the edge of the layout, and run another pair to plug-in panels located every 8 feet or so along the fascia. Even if you plan to use radio (wireless) throttles, run the wires to the "UTP" plug-in panels too, as batteries will fail. I plug the coiled cables that came with my North Coast Engineering cabs (throttles) into the panels so they'll be near at hand if someone's radio battery dies.

DCC offers myriad advantages. You can run an almost unlimited number of locomotives or multiple-locomotive consists at the same time, each independently controlled. You avoid the complexities of block wiring, although it is a good idea to subdivide the railroad into power districts, each powered by the command station or a booster (subdividing power districts by electronic circuit breakers is sufficient for small railroads). This makes it easier and quicker to troubleshoot electrical problems.

You also gain constant-on head-lights, Mars-type lights, beacons, and car interior lighting. Sound decoders have become extremely popular and are available to replicate the sound of almost every type of steam and diesel locomotive. Today, most locomotives are available with DCC sound decoders

An aluminum channel (designed to dress up the edges of ¾" plywood) can form the core of most deck-girder bridges. The girders are then strictly cosmetic, and work on supporting abutments, towers, bents, or piers can wait for another day.

factory-installed, which can be a huge time saver.

Installing a basic DCC system is very simple and quick. I'll use NCE's PowerCab as an example, 20: Run a pair of bus wires along the front of the railroad, then drop a feeder from each rail to the appropriate bus wire. Connect the bus wires to a plug-in panel furnished with the PowerCab; layout wiring is done! Then plug in a small transformer, often called a "wall wart," into a 120VAC source and into the back of the panel. Plug the PowerCab (and a second throttle if needed) into the front of the panel and run your DCC-equipped locomotive. Layout wiring to the point of operation doesn't get much simpler and quicker than that!

If your railroad grows beyond the capabilities of the basic system, you can add a command station and even boosters as needed. Want a wireless (radio) system? Just add a radio base station. The PowerCab then becomes a standard plug-in (not wireless) throttle. It's also handy to use when testing a locomotive at the workbench. Nothing has been wasted in terms of time or investment.

The National Model Railroad Association (nmra.org), which sets DCC standards, has introduced a new concept called Layout Command

Control. The idea is to offload all of the digital traffic from the basic DCC system that is not related to locomotive control. If this continues to grow in popularity and support by manufacturers, we will be able to run an LCC bus around the layout and plug in everything from telephones to timed or sequenced structure lights and signaling systems. This will represent another considerable savings of time.

Building bridges

I mentioned laying the main line through the location of a future diamond crossing without stopping to take time to actually build the diamond. I do the same thing with bridges by building the subroadbed and roadbed through the future bridge site.

I build deck-girder bridges around a ¾" aluminum-channel core, 21. The plastic bridge components then become merely cosmetic and can be put on hold until I have time—often years later—for "scenic" projects.

From plywood to scenery and structures

With the basic structure of our railroads-to-be in place, let's move on to considering ways to build scenery and, in Chapter 6, structures more quickly without unduly sacrificing quality.

1 When this photo was taken, the lower deck of my HO railroad had most of the scenery in place, such as it is in rural Indiana. But the upper deck sported only a photo backdrop and green-painted foam. Along with the lighting (4100K "cool white" fluorescents), valance, fascia, and a couple of structures, the scene looks reasonably complete. At this stage, time could better be spent on more important tasks elsewhere.

CHAPTER FIVE

Doing scenery in layers

Since the not-so-good old days when a coat of paint, a smear of white glue, and a dusting of green sawdust constituted a bona fide attempt at doing ground cover, a cornucopia of excellent scenery-making materials has blossomed onto the market. For the purposes of this book, we'll not spend much time on what are regarded as state-of-the-art scenic techniques but rather discuss ways to speed up the process one step at a time—or at least lead the viewer into thinking we have more done than we actually do, **1**.

Doug Leffler built an HO freelanced short line, the Lenawee Central, that was closely based on a local prototype short line, the Lenawee County. He observed that finishing the scenery in one location motivated him to move on to the next area. *Doug Leffler*

The Kudzu Principle

You may have heard of that invasive foreign vine called kudzu that is spreading over the Southeast like a rumpled blanket. I once asked a local how you plant kudzu, and he replied, "Throw it and run!" If only model railroad scenery were so easy to apply and quick to spread. But there is an element of the Southerner's comment that does apply to our modeling efforts. We'll call it the Kudzu Principle.

I'll share two different approaches that help to ensure that progress is made on the scenery front, a facet of layout construction that stops a surprising number of modelers dead in their tracks. The first approach, which incorporates the Kudzu Principle, was championed by Doug Leffler, a talented modeler who contributed regularly to *Railroad Model Craftsman* during my tenure as editor in the 1970s.

Doug found that he made more progress more quickly by fully scenicking one area of his HO small shortline railroad at a time, **2**. That looked so good that it motivated him to tackle the next section.

Bill Darnaby's HO scale Cleveland, Indianapolis, Cincinnati & St. Louis (the Maumee Route) has ten scale miles (600 feet) of main line, and Bill has been methodically working his way around it. At last report, he was down to the last 60 feet (a scale mile). His avoidance of building mock-ups or stand-ins is more efficient in the long run.

Bill used 2" foam board for the basic structure, **3**, which rests atop 1 x 2 brackets. He emphasizes that from the outset, the roadbed, track, and bordering ditches were in place, which gave the railroad a semi-finished appearance as operating crews ran trains along the main line. Adding finished scenery was made easier because the complete roadbed profile was already in place.

Bill built a large portion of the Midwest Railroad Modelers' HO layout in Batavia, Ill., and recalls that he "had no stomach for traditional riser, spline, screen wire, and plaster construction in my basement. Unless one has extreme patience to complete the scenery, he or she is faced with open benchwork when trains start to run."

Open benchwork isn't very attractive, so Bill decided to use 2" foam boards and hot-wire techniques to carve ditches, rivers, and so on. "This method provided ready-made platforms for the key structures such as depots and engine/yard terminals that I considered essential for train order operation."

Bill reports that 2" foam is rigid enough when placed on supports spaced 16" apart, especially when attached to the fascia. The backdrop material is inexpensive vinyl flooring that is flexible and cuts with a knife. "The back side takes paint very well, so as construction progressed, I painted the backdrop a sky blue and completed basic scenery: ditches, sub-roadbed, and ballast."

Bill started construction in January 1993, and he finished the 10 scale miles (plus staging) in five years. Another year was spent installing decoders (DCC was new), dispatcher's office, operators' desks, phones, depots, and train order signals. His first operating session was in February 1999; it was impossible to operate before then because the railroad was

3

Bill Darnaby's use of 2" foam for subroadbed and cork for the roadbed under Micro Engineering flextrack is shown in the under-construction photos at left, with 2019 views of the same areas at right. Note the weights holding the foam down while the foam-compatible glue set. Bill notes how flexible this method is: "Want a depression for a culvert? Just carve out the foam."

first built on both decks around the basement walls and then on both sides of the peninsula. As Bill has stated before, not having a television until the railroad was operational helped to ensure progress on the railroad.

"Lately, the railroad has reached the stage of completion that allows me to focus on landform scenery along the main line. The effect on me of the new scenery is remarkable," Bill recently observed. "It's like having a new railroad! The scenery also really adds to the effect of going somewhere—in effect, the layout becomes an actual railroad."

I found that I am more comfortable covering all "raw" foam and plywood surfaces with at least the first layer of ground cover as soon as practical. It's a quick way to give the impression the railroad is more finished than it actually is, especially with the fascia, valance, and overhead lighting in place. Just painting the plaster or foam landforms an olive-green color helps a lot, **1**. (We'll discuss using one color for the fascia, ground, and water shortly.)

Adding ground foam as a base coat costs time and money, but Randy Laframboise, who with Mike Sparks is building an outstanding HO tribute

to the former Rutland Railroad (see MRP 2016), agrees that the coating of ground foam is an important step: "I always apply ground foam first, as it provides something for the static grass to attach to. I have never obtained good results trying to apply it directly to a hard surface. Also, the ground foam provides a layer of undergrowth, which gives more depth to the grass and looks more realistic. I glue the ground foam with a 50/50 mix of Elmer's glue and water, then let dry before applying the static grass. I coat the area of ground foam to be covered with static grass with the thinned white glue and

David Barrow recommended painting the fascia and valance a "CTC machine green" color in MRP 1995, and I've used it ever since. I also use the color to paint ground cover and plaster-filled waterways. Paint-store formulas keep changing, but a scan of this sample will get you close enough.

apply the grass. I use undiluted glue on banks, hills, etc., as the grass has a tendency to flop over on inclines.

"The important step for success," Randy continued, "is to vacuum the static grass after 5 to 10 minutes. The suction of the vacuum pulls the fibers upright. If you get too close to the grass and suck up a patch, it's very easy to apply some hairspray and hit the area again with grass."

Painting everything green

We discussed painting the fascia and valance using latex paint mixed to resemble the olive-green used by Union Switch & Signal on their CTC panels in Chapter 4. But let's not stop there.

For those modeling "green country," which comprises most of North America, using a green hue to blend the fascia in with the scenery can save a lot of time. In the Midwest and large parts of Appalachia, and elsewhere, water—especially river water—is

often a muddy green-brown color, **4**. Coincidently, Union Switch & Signal's "CTC Machine Green" is very similar. I had a local paint store custom mix a batch based on a scan of a swatch.

So rather than spending time trying to avoid having the fascia color bleed into the adjoining scenery, I paint everything from landforms to watercourses with this satin-finish color. It looks good on the fascia, provides a good base for ground-covering materials such as ground foam and static grass, and is a near perfect hue for many waterways.

I must admit, however, that some scenes made using recent water-making products from Woodland Scenics look very impressive, **5**.

Trees and hillsides

When you want a really spectacular tree for a mini scene, such as a kid swinging on a tire tied to a rope in the front yard of a Victorian house, then

taking extra pains to make a really detailed tree is justified. A sagebrush armature is often a good place to start.

Poly-fiber-fill "puffball" trees still have their uses, **6**. In most mountain areas, we're modeling not individual trees but rather forest canopies. In such instances, spending the time and dollars to abut countless foreground-quality trees seems to me to be wasteful. The accompanying photo taken in central Appalachia shows that you can't see anything but leaves.

But when you need to create a grove of trees along the right-of-way, **7**, or a forest lining a mountain stream, you can't afford the luxury of spending that much time per tree.

Where the trunk and branch structure is likely to be visible, however, SuperTrees from Scenic Express coated with leaf flakes have become a favorite among modelers. But some of us insist on making the process more time-consuming than it needs to be.

One has to be open to new ideas. Woodland Scenics has continued to development its line of water-simulating products and has achieved some very impressive results. *Woodland Scenics*

In the May 2014 MR, I wrote about making a complete tree in under a minute. This does not include the time spent removing the curlicue "leaves" from inside the tree armature, but that can be done while watching TV. Beyond that, the process is simple:

First, round up the materials. You'll need a large carton of SuperTrees and several bags of one or two similarly colored leaf flakes. (Noticeably different leaf hues will create a salt-and-pepper effect.) You'll also need several spray cans of cheap, gooey hairspray and several more spray cans of a flat gray primer. (Tree trunks and branches are more often gray than brown.) Add a pair of work gloves, and find three low-side box tops like those that come on Walthers structure kits and arrange them in a row in your garage or outdoors if it's not too windy.

From your stash of SuperTree armatures, pick one. If the top is bent over, snap it off; you now have two trees. (You can straighten the "truck"

using a soldering iron, but we're in a hurry here, remember?) Hold an armature in one hand and spray it gray over the first box to avoid painting something else. Then immediately coat the armature with hair spray.

Move the armature over the second box, which is filled with leaf flakes. Coat it with leaf flakes but not too liberally; airiness is a virtue.

Toss the coated tree into the third box, knocking off some of the leaf slakes, which we'll reuse. Done! And only 30 seconds or so have expired.

Don't toss out anything, as the fine bits that are left over make great weeds and shrubs. And some of the best SuperTree armatures can be left uncoated and used as yellow/orange-hued autumn trees.

Speaking of uncoated SuperTree armatures, when Ted Pamperin told me that he was going to model the Chesapeake & Ohio and Mann's Creek railroads' New River Valley of West Virginia and depict it in the autumn

when the foliage was off the trees, I thought he had bitten off more than he could easily chew. Boy, was I wrong! Ted is one of the more innovative modelers I know, and he developed a technique for doing realistic leaf-less deciduous trees quickly using SuperTree armatures.

Better still, he pre-plants them in 2" foam panels, wildly sprays on an assortment of autumnal colors outdoors, and then drops in the panels at a steep angle to create mountain slopes, **8**. He can cover one side of a peninsula in the time it takes most of us to add leaf flakes to SuperTree armatures.

"Clothshell" scenery

You've no doubt read about former MR editor Linn Westcott's "hardshell" scenery using Hydrocal plaster covered by what he called "zip texturing." Gregg Condon, who models in HOn3, developed a technique he calls "clothshell scenery," **8-8**.

6

"Puffball" trees made from poly-fiber fill (top) aren't meant to be trees at all but rather the tops of a dense deciduous forest canopy. They still do a credible job when modeling the verdant Appalachians (here at Haysi/Berta, Va., on the Clinchfield, above) where tree trunks and branches are all but invisible.

"Oh, yes, clothshell saves time!" Gregg responded to my inquiry. "I've done a few NMRA convention demos of it using a small framework of insulation foam about the size of a sheet of paper. The edges were curvy, the top open. I put a piece of pre-cut cloth (worn-out blankets and old towels) onto a clipboard and held it up where the audience could see it, gave it a couple squeezes of Liquid Nails from a caulk gun, spread it with a putty knife, and slapped it onto the foam framework."

Of Gregg's extensive list of timesavers (Chapter 8), he counts this as number one. There are only two materials to gather—construction adhesive and a piece of cloth—and only two tools are needed—scissors and putty knife. "There's nothing to mix, nothing to drip, and nothing to clean up but a putty knife and fingertips!" he concluded.

Photo backdrops

Photo backdrops, be they commercial or homemade, have finally assumed

their rightful place at the top of the choices when it comes to extending a scene, often to infinity. But there are some pitfalls and opportunities that lie along the way we should discuss.

Almost all of the photo backdrops lining my relatively narrow (16" to 24" except in one yard) HO railroad were produced by SceniKing (sceniking. com), **9**. Specific scenes in small towns comprise a mix of SceniKing and my own digital photos, **10**, the latter backdated using Photoshop Elements software. PSE is inexpensive, it's easy

7

Scenic Express SuperTrees are a quick way to create a line of trees along the right-of-way. I clean off the curlicue leaves, spray them with gray primer and immediately with thick hair spray, and coat them with leaf flakes. Time per tree after the curlicues are moved (while watching TV) is about 30 seconds.

to learn the basics, there's lots of rail-oriented online help, and it will save you a ton of time.

Often your backdrop will extend higher than the top of the photo you're using for ground-level scenery. Removing the sky portion of the photo solves this problem. When doing this with a new no. 11 hobby-knife blade, it's easy to cut a neat line around hard edges like structure roofs and smoke stacks.

When cutting along a tree line, however, cut perhaps 1/16" into the

foliage to avoid any hint of the sky showing above the trees. And if you're using the same series of backdrop photos butted end-to-end to extend a scene, cut more deeply into the foliage to reshape it, **11**. This avoids seeing the same grove of trees pop up every four feet or so. Similarly, I section out any distinctive buildings such as a particular barn or house when abutting the same sequence of backdrop photo panels.

I have yet to find the perfect adhesive to use when attaching photo

backdrops to a hard surface. Elmer's white glue works pretty well, but I now see some edges coming loose. Ailene's Tacky Glue seems to be doing a good job of repairing the loose backdrop photos, so maybe I should have used it from the start. I tried some highly touted spray adhesives with disappointing results. I did not try wallpaper paste.

I used LARC Products peel-and-stick photo backdrops for an O scale project railroad with excellent results. But however you use photo backdrops,

8

Ted Pamperin had to cover entire mountainsides with trees after their leaves had fallen. His did this quickly and effectively with SuperTrees that were stuck into foam panels and sprayed with a variety of autumn hues. The panels were then tilted into the benchwork. Done! *Four photos: Ted Pamperin*

they will go up much faster than hand-painting the scenery.

You can avoid a clash between a 3-D model, especially a building flat, and a 2-D photo backdrop by setting up the same model walls in the needed position and photographing them. Then use a print of that image as the backdrop that adjoins the 3-D structure.

Kinko's, Staples, Walgreens, Wal-Mart, and so on can make poster-size prints for use as backdrop images. They're careful not to allow copyright infringements, so bringing a model with you to show them what you need and why may pave the way.

Ditches, crops, fields, and roads

Prototype railroads are extremely vigilant in provide adequate drainage. So modeling a right-of-way simply by plopping down some roadbed and track is unlikely to create a realistic roadbed profile.

I model the Midwestern plains, although in many areas they're not as flat as one might assume. As I described in the July 2013 MR, after trying various techniques to raise the land along the right-of-way, I settled upon ⅜"-thick foam board to create the field side of ditches, **12**. This also makes it quick and easy to plant JTT cornstalks, **13**. Plastic cornstalks, wheat fields, and rows of soybeans are simply glued atop the foam sheets, **14**. Cutting a recess for a building foundation is also easy.

Wheat fields can be modeled with mats or by applying electrostatic

I used SceniKing (sceniking.com) photo backdrops for most areas of my relatively narrow (16" to 24" in rural areas) shelf railroad. They vastly extend the apparent distance to the horizon on my flatlands railroad. Most popular scenes are now available in 16½" by 72" Rollouts.

grass. Don't let the latter technique intimidate you. With a good applicator and a supply of various hues of grass material, by applying grass to perhaps a square foot at a time, you can cover larger areas rather quickly. You can increase the depth of the grass by applying thick hairspray to the dried and vacuumed first layer, and then applying a second layer of grass fibers atop the first. Try it!

Alternatively, Scenic Express sells a see-through grass-like mat that covers large areas quickly, **15**.

I discovered that a product called Elastomeric Custom Patch Smooth, which I found in quart containers at Lowe's, makes a good base for roads of all types, **16**. The top surface has to be "floated" like concrete using water and a palette knife, but it goes down quickly. After drying, some cracks may appear, but they can be filled by rubbing more patch material into the cracks.

Wide-open spaces

Randy Laframboise echoes my own experience that when you plan for more open spaces, **17**, you get more layout built faster. He cited the benefits of modeling open spaces as not just the time savings but also the increased openness and breathing room it provides in the overall layout experience. "Unless you are modeling

In towns, wherever possible I took photos of needed scenes and used Photoshop Elements to remove modern giveaways such as vehicles, red STOP signs, green street signs, and store signage ("Diet Coke") for my railroad set in 1954. I should have added vehicles appropriate for the period, however. Dullcote helps to protect the backdrop prints during later scenery applications.

There are at least two identical SceniKing background kits butted end-to-end in this photo. Reshaping the trees while trimming off the sky—which won't be high enough for backdrops more than 16" tall—disguises the repetition. Eye-catchers such as farms and houses can be sectioned out of the backdrop or hidden behind tall trees, low hills, or 3-D structures.

I use folded 24" x 48" panels of ⅜" insulating foam available at big-box stores to raise the field side of ditches. I staple or glue down strips of foam, then cut the sloping ditch edge with a package knife. The adjacent main line sits ½" above the subroadbed.

JTT cornstalks, available from Model Rectifier (left), have a wire core that is easily inserted into the ⅜" foam I use to quickly "plant" the fields along the right-of-way. Planting stalks one at a time goes quickly. Busch makes rows of cornstalks, shown at right after being painted an ochre color. Bluford Shops also sells interlocking rows of corn in green and ochre.

A SceniKing backdrop, JTT cornstalks, a wheat-colored mat from Scenic Express, and rows of soybeans made from brown pipe cleaners (obtained online) coated with gooey hairspray and leaf flakes (a technique developed by Jason Klocke) are all visible in this scene east of Metcalf, Ill., on my railroad. All of these products allow fields to be modeled quickly.

city or industrial areas," he suggests, "including more open areas will not only save time and money but also make your layout seem larger and more balanced, even at the expense of possibly having to delete one or more towns from your wish list."

Moreover, ensuring separation between towns is important. "I do not want a train being in two towns at once," he stated. "It destroys the feeling of actually going somewhere, making realistic operations impossible."

Structure building tips

With timesaving landform techniques in hand, let's move on to finding ways to save time where structures are concerned.

Scenic Express sells Heki's "WildGras" see-through grass mat. It allows large areas like fields to be quickly covered with deep grass that looks much like a multi-layer coating of static grass. It's an example of spending more money to save time.

I used Elastomeric Custom Patch Smooth purchased at Lowe's to build up roads. The top surface has to be floated (wetted) and smoothed with a palette knife. The backdrop comprises recent photos of 2nd Street in Veedersburg, Ind., with modern additions, vehicles, and signs removed using Photoshop Elements.

17 Planning for open spaces, as is evident on the HO scale Rutland layout built by Randy Laframboise and Mike Sparks, helps to get more layout built more quickly, as they are devoid of time-consuming structures. "The benefits of modeling open spaces are not just the time savings but also the increased openness and breathing room it provides in the overall layout experience," he stresses.

CHAPTER SIX

Time-saving structure tips

1

Perry Squier kitbashed the main structure of the Empire Sash & Door Co. at Friendship, N.Y., from Atlas Middlesex Manufacturing Co. kits. He worked from photos and footprint dimensions obtained from Sanborn fire-insurance and government valuation maps to build this remarkably accurate model.

We have to choose our battles if we want to save time and other resources. If you're a dedicated structure modeler, our discussion in this chapter may not meet your needs. But if you're also concerned about getting your model railroad built, scenicked, and operating within a reasonable timeframe, you may find some tips here that allow you to enjoy your favorite aspects of our hobby without consuming precious time on projects of less importance and prominence.

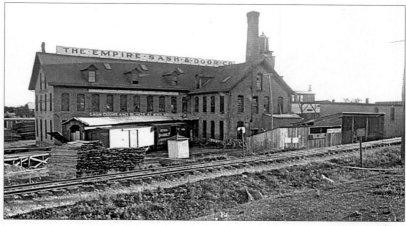

Creative kitbashing

Kitbashing, a term coined by Dave Frary and Bob Hayden back in the 1960s, is a popular and often timesaving way to build structures. But there's a bit more to it than simply combining this with that for whatever reason. A balance between saving time and achieving realism is important.

An excellent example is Perry Squier's superbly executed model of the Empire Sash & Door Co., a structure once located along the Pittsburg, Shawmut & Northern in Friendship, N.Y., **1**. Using walls from the Atlas Middlesex Manufacturing Co. HO kit (150-721) saved time without unduly compromising the realism of the finished model.

Moreover, there's something about having actual structure parts in your hand when you're kitbashing a model. It's easier to visualize the path ahead. You can also make photocopies of walls and cut and paste them together to be sure your plans are feasible before cutting and rearranging parts.

I'll share with you a good example of saving time by spending a little more of it the first time around. I needed a model of the wood interlocking tower that once graced the southeast corner of the Nickel Plate Road–Chicago & Eastern Illinois diamonds at my former hometown, Cayuga, Ind. I spent many hours "helping" the towerman line up routes and post train orders, so it's an important model for my HO edition of the NKP's St. Louis line through Cayuga.

I noticed that a Walthers interlocking tower kit (933-3071) looked a lot like the Cayuga tower. By moving the chimney and relocating one wall, I could come pretty close. Moreover, I never have found a photo showing whether the second-story west side windows were as built or partially boarded up, as was the case on two other sides. So I felt more comfortable kitbashing it rather than going to the trouble of scratchbuilding what could turn out to be an inaccurate model.

The project went well after I made a new roof, but I decided not to section out the chimney base. It was only when I tried to replicate a low-angle shot of Berkshire 707 and a compatriot passing the tower that the extra length of the tower started to bother me. I therefore

2 I lacked information on the west wall of the tower at Cayuga, Ind. (top) where I spent many hours in my youth, so I kitbashed it from a similar Walthers tower kit (middle). But I neglected to section out the chimney base, which made the tower too wide. Over time, this gnawed on me, so I did it over again (bottom).

gave the tower to a friend who models the C&EI, found another kit, and did a better job the second time around. The time I saved initially was more than lost when I wound up building a second tower, **2**.

I had better luck the first time around when I kitbashed a large B&O tower into a more compact C&O "cabin," **3**.

I asked U.K. modeler Brian Moore, who models the Southern Pacific in the steam–diesel transition era around Guadalupe, Calif., about how he saves time building structures for his HO railroad.

"I've learned that, to get anywhere, even—or especially—when attempting to model a prototype, you have to accept compromise and let some stuff go. The overriding reason for building my layout is to operate trains, not to build a 100-percent-accurate diorama. Not only do the structures I've built 'look the part' but they were also easy enough to put together using bits from a couple of Walthers' Clayton County Lumber kits, plus some simple scratchbuilding," Brian replied. One warehouse structure had a unique top story attached, **4**. Modeling that turned an anonymous group of buildings into a signature structure of the area he's modeling.

"I spent a lot more time on the Guadalupe and Oceano depots," Brian recalled, "as they are true 'signature structures' and both much-modified AMB laser kits. Anyone reasonably familiar with Guadalupe, **5**, would recognize depot-deviation in a flash, so I consulted a lot of pictures when building it. Fortunately, and sometimes unfortunately, there are many more photos of depots than the anonymous buildings that surround them."

Hiding heritage
Kitbashing is also a good way to disguise the heritage of a model, even if the finished structure is entirely freelanced. I suspect we've all seen more than our share of popular kits built precisely to the kit instructions, including paint and signs.

If that kit happens to be a model of an actual structure on the railroad

This AHM kit (since sold by different suppliers), for a large B&O tower had the bones I needed to kitbash it into a smaller C&O "cabin" for the Allegheny Midland. This required narrowing the lower walls, using styrene strips for the upper-story windows, and building a new roof. Many such structures are now available as laser kits.

3

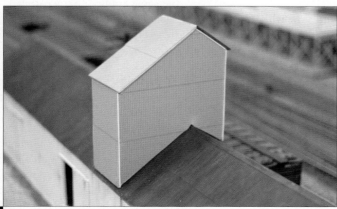

United Kingdom modeler Brian Moore kitbashed two Walthers' Clayton County Lumber kits "plus some simple scratchbuilding" to create a good-enough model of the Western Packing Co. warehouse in Guadalupe, Calif. One warehouse structure had a unique top story, which makes the complex easily identifiable to anyone familiar with the area. *Two photos: Brian Moore*

4

5

segment you're modeling, as was approximately the case with Brian Moore's two SP depots, consider yourself blessed. Otherwise, it will distract and detract from the realism of a scene by being too familiar ("Nice job on the Revell enginehouse!") or clearly a well-known structure that belongs on another railroad.

Using inexpensive kits as place-holders is another way to make a railroad look more finished than it actually is until the correct structure can be kitbashed or scratchbuilt, 3-5 and 6. Yes, in the long run it's a waste of time and money, but it may motivate you to get more done on the railroad as it begins to look finished.

Avoiding structure-heavy areas

Famed modeler John Allen was quoted as saying that modeling mountains was enjoyable, but modeling city buildings could be tedious and slow with all the windows and details. I now model the rural Midwest—west-central Indiana and east-central Illinois to be more precise. My railroad runs from one modestly sized city—Frankfort, Ind.—to another—Charleston, Ill. In neither case did it make a big deal about the structures that lined the tracks.

Between those activity hubs, the railroad plied the farmlands that feed our nation. It traversed far more miles out-of-town than in-town. Even in town, 7, there were few structures

lining the tracks. That alone saved me a lot of structure-building time, and it allowed me more time to focus on key structures.

The same applied to my earlier Appalachian-climbing Allegheny Midland layout—lots of trees but few structures, 8.

Flats and low-relief structures

The meager area we have to work with when we build our railroads must be consumed judiciously. Similarly, we have limited time and funds for hobby endeavors. One way to save on all three fronts is to use building flats and/or low-relief structures.

True, using a building flat or only the first inch or two of a structure

84

An AMB laser kit was the basis for Brian Moore's highly detailed HO model. Confining the scope of a layout to a few such scenes allows time to do them well. *Brian Moore*

Photos for building sides

Lance Mindheim has mastered the technique of making realistic structures using a core of styrene "wallpapered" with photo laminates of the actual prototype, **12**. Using digital photos, usually adjusted to correct unwanted perspective using photo-editing software such as Photoshop Elements, saves time adding details, texture, and weathering to a model and achieves unsurpassed realism.

In the May 2012 MR, Paul Dolkos discussed using photos to model a structure's exterior. He calls this technique "photo veneer." The photos capture not only the structure's exterior and weathering but also myriad details such as address numbers, cracks in the wall, and curtains.

Paul uses Photoshop software to size images to scale and adjust them to create the desired model structure facade. For freelanced or selectively compressed structures, he modifies images to include more or fewer windows, doors, and other features. For a structure where all walls are visible, Paul notes he sometimes has to adapt the "good" images to stand in for the walls that can't be photographed or are in shadow.

"Once I have the set up desired structure images," Paul reports, "I print them on paper. Ordinary bond paper has worked for me, but other weights or surfaces may be better for special situations."

The photos in **13** show the construction sequence for Paul's technique. "Don't use cardstock too thick or too thin," Paul cautions. "A scale 6" depth for a window opening looks good. I add 3-D elements to the structure like chimneys, vents, and cornices. Upon completion, I spray the model with Dullcote to protect it from water runs, particularly with ink-jet images."

I used some of Lance's and Paul's techniques to model the Fable House Hotel behind the Cayuga, Ind., depot, **14**. The depot is long gone, but the hotel still stands, so I was able to photograph all four sides.

But two of the sides were in shadow, and the sunny sides had boarded-up windows. I retouched a few

creates some scenic compromises, **9**. But this also allows you to model the trackside wall of a structure to scale in a minimum of benchwork width. Moreover, my main goal is not to build models just for the sake of building models but rather to support the function of the railroad. So if I can squeeze a grain elevator or even a massive soybean plant, **10**, into a narrow space, I'm very happy to employ a flat or low-relief building.

Building the soybean plant silos only half their full depth was beneficial in another way: I could use the molding for the back half of the silos to double the number of silos. That

often works on other structures that are built as flats or low-relief buildings by using the unused rear and perhaps side walls to extend the trackside wall. Even on full 3-D structures, if the wall away from the aisle can't be seen, save it for use on another project.

This is helpful on both the backdrop and aisle sides of the main line. Just a hint—perhaps a loading platform, **11**—of an unmodeled structure will provide the visual clue your operators will need to know where to spot a car.

For more tips on blending structures to scenes, please see my book, *Space-saving Industries for Your Railroad* (Kalmbach, 2016).

6 Randy Laframboise used a Walthers water tank as a stand-in—for 10 years!—for one he is now scratchbuilding. *Randy Laframboise*

7 The NKP and B&O tracks skirted downtown Metcalf, Ill., and I haven't found any photos of the commercial structures nearest the tracks. So reasonable guesses based on a Sanborn fire-insurance map and compression due to lack of space will have to do unless better information surfaces.

windows using Photoshop Elements photo-editing software and pasted them over the blanked-off window openings. I bonded the photo-paper sides to a .060" styrene core, glued on windowsills made from strip styrene to give the walls a bit of texture, and added a fabricated roof and porch. Other than the window sills, the only

"details" are flower boxes made from a piece of strip styrene with some colored bits of foam glued on top and overstuffed couches and chairs on the porch.

I saved a lot of time and effort by not cutting out the window openings and adding styrene window moldings to the wall itself.

Using time-saving products

I make liberal use of time-saving products like quick-drying Plastruct solvents, acrylic paint, and PanPastels.

For example, my standard approach to painting a brick building is to spray on the appropriate (brick red or buff as a rule) flat primer from a rattle can and then rub the surface with a similar

Like most mountain-climbing railroads, the Allegheny Midland followed waterways that had cut narrow valleys through high ridges. Scenery therefore comprised a lot more forest canopy than downtown structures, which saved both time and money, as sacks of poly-fiber "puffballs" could be made while watching TV.

The towering concrete grain elevator at Oakland, Ill., had to be reduced in scope and made as a flat because the 16"-wide benchwork depth precluded modeling the back half of the silos. But one's attention is focused on the unloading shed during operating sessions.

To save construction time compared to scratchbuilding the Swift soybean plant at Frankfort, Ind. (the prototype photo shows more recent additions), I used Walthers' Valley Cement kit silos (here used as flats, allowing the rear half to double the number of silos) and corrugated structure parts to build other segments.

10

Even with 24" of depth to work with, I didn't have room for the two main tracks, depot, and freight house in Frankfort, Ind. The loading platform tips off the switching crew as to the freight house's location. A quickly constructed narrow platform thus does the same "work" as building a model of a complete industrial building.

11

A lone boxcar sits outside of Family & Son on Lance Mindheim's Downtown Spur HO layout, set in Miami in 2008. The structure is a .060" styrene core "wallpapered" with photo laminates of the prototype. Stand-off details such as gutters and conduits were then added to create a sense of depth. Track is Micro Engineering code 70 with joint bars and airbrushed with Earth Brown followed by a dusting of burnt umber. Ties were airbrushed a faded gray and given a wash with burnt umber artist oils. After the track was laid and ballasted, the rails were masked and Heki Prairie Grass static grass applied. *Lance Mindheim*

color of PanPastels. I hesitate to call it weathering powder or pastel chalk, even though the latter is its primary market. It contains an adhesive that bonds it nicely to any matte surface, and I never overspray it with Dullcote.

(See Chapter 7 for more on using PanPastels to save an incredible amount of modeling time.)

Some structures that are needed to establish a specific scene are worth the time it takes to scratchbuild them. This is especially true when the structure is well known, if only by you. We call these "signature" structures, and they can help to establish signature scenes around which the entire premise of a model railroad is designed and constructed. The satisfaction derived from seeing a familiar landmark come back to life, if only in miniature, is not to be underestimated. This is doubly true if the scene no longer exists.

But scratchbuilding a key structure may not consume much time at all, thanks to the modeling materials and tools we have at our disposal today. And, as I often remark in my clinics at NMRA conventions and Railroad Prototype Modelers conferences, scratchbuilding is often easier than building a similar kit in that you don't even have to read the instructions!

The stuff that moves

Railroading and hence scale model railroading is all about movement, so let's shift our focus to saving time and effort while building up a roster of locomotives and cars in Chapter 7.

Paul Dolkos also makes excellent use of the photo-lamination technique. Paul tapes the structure image to a piece of illustration board that will form the core of the building, and he cuts out the window and door openings. This leaves score marks on the board, providing a guide so they can be cut out accurately; he includes some extra wall material for ease of handling. Paul touches up exposed edges around the wall openings, and an identical print of the exterior is glued on the backside of the wall piece with the windows and doors showing through. *Two photos: Paul Dolkos*

I borrowed a page from Lance and Paul's modeling notebook and speeded up construction by backdating photos of the still-standing Fable House hotel in Cayuga, Ind., then gluing them to a core of .060" styrene. The roof and porch were conventionally scratchbuilt. The hotel sits well back from the aisle.

1

CHAPTER SEVEN

Improving engines & rolling stock

I can't get Nickel Plate-prototype Consolidations, and no suitable "donor" locomotives are available. So some running-board stripes and NKP decals applied to stock Bachmann 2-8-0s will have to suffice. At least for now, they look just fine strutting their stuff as they go about their daily toil. Here no. 908 struggles up Cayuga Hill as it crosses the steel viaduct over the Little Vermilion River near Humrick, Ill.

A modeler can contentedly spend a year building and detailing a locomotive. Indeed, building or superdetailing a relatively few stunning models can become the main objective. Many O fine-scale (Proto:48) modelers enjoy scratchbuilding and/or superdetailing locomotives, rolling stock, and track almost to the exclusion of realistically operating railroads. But our objective here is to find ways to populate our railroads with something other than out-of-the-box models without spending a lot of time doing that.

Using stand-ins

Much as I'd love to have a small fleet of the Nickel Plate Road's high-set ex-Clover Leaf 2-8-0s, nothing close is presently available. Bachmann makes a good-looking, good-running Consolidation based on the Illinois Central's beefy 2-8-0s, which had rather tall drivers for this type of engine. Fortunately, most of the more prominent details look generic. I therefore decided that a trio of those models, **1**, would be a fine addition to the NKP's roster until the day when more accurate models are available, perhaps as a 3-D printing project.

Placeholders are often used for buildings, so I see no great harm in doing the same thing with steam locomotives. Few of my operating crew are familiar enough with NKP Consolidations for it to be a noteworthy visual offense.

Look to the USRA fleet

Frank Hodina has long been intrigued by the Chicago & Illinois Midland. He felt a little constrained by the demands of strict prototype modeling, so he and Jeff Halloin looked to a C&IM predecessor, the Chicago & Illinois Western, which—as he explained in *Model Railroad Planning* 2008—gave him the leeway he felt he needed. They assumed the C&IW had survived on its own and developed that theme with locomotives and cars that, at a glance, looked like C&IM prototypes.

Fortunately, the C&IM had USRA-design steam locomotives. Equally fortunately, Like-Like's (now Walthers') Proto 2000 line includes USRA 2-10-2s. A little detail work and some custom decals created the needed steam roster, **2**.

In the West, the Harriman Common Standards for motive power and rolling stock also serve as a design platform to work from. Adding a Vanderbilt tender to a Bachmann Consolidation would be a good start, but U.K. modeler Brian Moore took it well beyond that mark with a stunning array of new details, **3**.

As larger, more modern power joined the rosters of Class 1 railroads, USRA and Harriman engines tended to hold their own right to the end of steam. Some migrated to short lines.

Kitbash what you need

Sometimes more than adding detail and swapping tenders is needed to

The USRA's WWI designs for a variety of light and heavy steam locomotives were, without exception, good-looking and capable machines. They were assigned to many railroads, which makes them excellent candidates for freelanced railroad rosters. Frank Hodina detailed this HO Proto 2000 2-10-2 for his freelanced Chicago & Illinois Western to resemble those of base-prototype Chicago & Illinois Midland. Number 705 is a Proto 2000 USRA heavy 2-10-2. Most details are brass castings. *Frank Hodina*

3

achieve a desired outcome. Adding a lead truck to a switcher has been done on full-size locomotives, but here's an example of removing the lead truck to create a distinctive piece of motive power.

John Glaab kitbashed a Bachmann 2-8-0 into an 0-8-0 for his Magarac Steel & Iron HO layout. A hefty 0-8-0 was needed to handle ladle cars. Following the B&O's example, he converted the 2-8-0 to an 0-8-0, **4**.

If a desired locomotive is not available for the railroad you plan to model, but you have found a way to kitbash a commercially available engine, remember that this will take time away from layout construction. That may be a perfectly acceptable tradeoff, but it has to be figured into the overall plan if the start date for operations or the total time commitment is a consideration.

John also notes that "The steep decline in the price of old brass may be a blessing in disguise. You can now find very good locos for less than $100. With a motor and probably gearbox change plus a DCC decoder, you can have a fine-running steam engine that will cost you about one-third of the price of a new plastic or die-cast model. This will encourage more kitbashing."

Weathering steam locomotives

Weathering a well-detailed commercial model of a steam locomotive is a project that many modelers would consider a bit daunting, **5**. As I reported in the November 2013 MR, I did just that in just over seven minutes.

I won't go into detail again here, but the process is very simple using PanPastels. I chose various grays from off white to charcoal to add steaks from soot, water deposits, and road grime. The factory finish on the model has sufficient grit to secure the PanPastels; lacking that, I would have sprayed the model with Dullcote before applying the PanPastels.

No final overspray is needed if PanPastels are applied to a rough-texture surface. I handle a high percentage of my steam fleet at least once between operating sessions while re-staging the "muzzle-loading" (stub-ended) staging yards, which requires

4

John Glaab reports that the conversion of a Bachmann 2-8-0 into an 0-8-0, a la B&O practice, went fairly fast: He removed the lead truck, shortened the pilot, and added an air tank on the pilot as well as a second sand dome and air pump. A clear-vision tender was called for, so John shortened an old AHM/Rivarossi Indiana Harbor Belt tender to fit on the Bachmann tender frame.

Brian Moore models the Guadalupe Sub of the Southern Pacific's Coast Division in 1954 when most local freights were hauled by 2-8-0s. Brass being beyond his budget, he used Bachmann's Consolidation to create "close enough" versions. SP 2581 has a reworked front end and cylinders, simplified valve gear, modified piping and handrails around the smoke box, new front dome, and a Bachmann coal Vanderbilt tender converted to oil. *Brian Moore*

I used PanPastels colors and foam applicators to weather this out-of-the-box Proto 2000 Berkshire in just over 7 minutes and 13 seconds. It's no contest winner but will fit right in among a fleet of Proto 2000 Berkshires after it gets a Mars light and a cracked sleeve on the last driver pair is replaced (note the side rod angles downward).

5

6

You can spend an hour or more applying a great weathering job to a diesel with a variety of materials. To save time, Dullcote sprayed from a can will provide enough texture for PanPastels. If you later have time to go back and do a more thorough job, the weathering will wash off. But it has enough grip with no clear coat for normal handling not to affect it.

7

When Jim Six weathered these relatively new (in my modeled era) Atlas GP7s, he used a light touch but removed the "plastic sheen." Remember that we're theoretically viewing our models through a hundred or more feet of atmosphere, which on the prototype reduces the apparent shininess of a painted surface. Military and large-scale vehicle modelers perfected this long ago.

turning steam locomotives end-for-end, and I have yet to reapply PanPastels.

The process for weathering a diesel, **6**, is similar and takes even less time. Even relatively new (according to their built date and the era you model) diesels look better when their have a flat finish and light weathering, **7**.

Caboose and freight car weathering

Weathering freight cars that have a dull finish is also a quick and easy task, **8**, as is killing the shine on metal wheels, **9**. Accurail's factory-applied paint is almost an ideal surface on which to apply PanPastels. For cars with a shiny or even eggshell surface, a quick spray with Dullcote provides a good weathering surface.

If you spend more than a minute weathering a freight car, you're making a sub-hobby out of weathering—an often-rewarding task best left for after the railroad is fully operational.

During a photo shoot, I noticed a factory-painted brass caboose was a bit too shiny even for a car right out of the paint shop. I lifted it off the rails and used a charcoal PanPastel color to add some soot streaks from the

During a video shoot where unweathered cars stood out, I aged several—including this Accurail single-sheathed boxcar—in about a minute per car using PanPastels. For most, a color range from white to black and rust to Tuscan red will suffice.

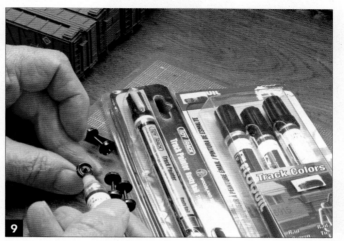

Paint in felt-tip pens makes dulling metal wheels easy. Rotate the wheel-set between your fingers as the paint flows. I use Rail Tie Brown for most cars; modern wheels are often a rust color. This can be done without removing the wheels from the truck frame.

As yet another deadline loomed during a photo shoot, I used PanPastels to add some grime to a "wood" caboose. I also darkened the wheels using a felt-tip weathering pen without removing the wheelsets from the truck sideframes. It took only a minute or two and gave the aging caboose the desired "ridden hard and put away wet" appearance.

wood-burning stove and a tan color to simulate dust kicked up as the caboose rumbles along the high iron, **10**.

Many veteran operators and clubs require all cars to be equipped with metal wheels and couplers. The slight extra time spent converting nonconforming cars will be repaid many times over, as the metal wheels not only roll much more freely, thus allowing longer trains, but also are less prone to accumulate dirt on the wheel treads that must be cleaned off. And

Kadee metal couplers, also a standard for many clubs, also require less maintenance and perform very reliably. I've been especially pleased the newer type with the "whisker" centering springs.

A caveat: When planning a railroad that includes grades, it's wise to keep track in switching areas dead level. Those metal wheelsets really do roll freely!

If I notice that some wheels have accumulated dirt, usually causing the car to shimmy, I flip the car upside

down in a foam holder and rub the tread using a soft-lead pencil. This quickly scrapes off the grunge while polishing the wheels. This doesn't happen often with polished metal wheels, however.

Passenger cars certainly received a lot more tender loving care than freight cars, as they were often washed by hand or mechanical washers between runs. But neither hand-held brushes nor mechanical washers always reached the roofs. On Nickel Plate passenger cars, the blue-painted roofs often appeared to have been painted black or were covered with a patina of rust.

Fortunately, Walthers makes very nice models of NKP lightweight coaches and 10-6 Pullmans, but the finish is not gritty enough to secure the PanPastels. Masking off the roof and spraying it with Dullcote prior to adding charcoal- and/or rust-colored PanPastels solves that problem, **11**.

Painting models

I own a very nice spray booth with twin exhaust fans, and I also have both single- and double-action airbrushes. But for individual models, either structures or rolling stock, I often use spray cans to save time, even for a four-color caboose, **12**. Not counting paint-drying time, the entire process actually consumed only a few minutes, including applying the masking tape for the stripe. There was no paint to thin or airbrush to tune up and clean.

After adding decals to the glossy red and gray sides, I sprayed it with Dullcote and weathered it using PanPastels.

Making do for now

My good friend Bill Darnaby has one of the most impressive rosters of rolling stock you'll find anywhere. But it wasn't always up to his current standards, which include metal wheels and no molded-on grab irons or ladders. His initial goal was to get the railroad running, and the older, less-detailed cars served that purpose nicely.

"Actually, I still use a handful of rather ancient Athearn 'blue-box' cars," Bill reports. "They are the faceless fleet of black two-bay hoppers that slosh

11 NKP's lightweight passenger car roofs were painted blue, but the car-washing brushes cleaned only the sides. A quick spray of Dullcote and some PanPastel colors killed the shiny roofs and made it easy to add a sooty or rusty hue.

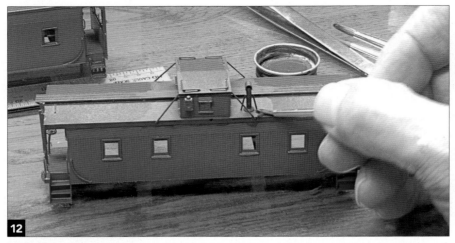

12 NKP cabooses sported four colors: bright red sides, a light gray stripe along the roof eaves, black roofs and underbodies, and freight car brown end platforms and steps. I used "rattle cans" to spray the separate bottom black and the sides gray; masked off the eave stripe and sprayed everything red, and then brush-painted the roofs black and the ends freight car brown.

back and forth in coal service from the mines on the Third Sub to the docks in Toledo. I can't justify Kadee's nicely detailed twins for that service."

I started on my current railroad a decade or so later than Bill, so I was quite happy to relieve him of those older models, which were equipped with the essentials—Kadee metal couplers, InterMountain metal wheels, and weathering—at a modest price. Now I'm starting to upgrade my own roster. I'm sure the displaced Darnaby-built and -weathered cars will find new homes.

Mass production

This is one of those "Do-as-I-say, not do-as-I-do" situations like the one I described in Chapter 4. When Perry Squier needed 32 log-carrying flat cars, **13**, he cut all of the various sizes of stripwood and then mass-assembled them in a manner that would have made Henry Ford jump for joy.

Me? I probably would have cut the wood needed for each car and assembled it before I lost interest. The moral of the story is to gang up projects that require multiple copies. It may occasionally be a grind, but you'll get a lot more done in a minimum amount of time.

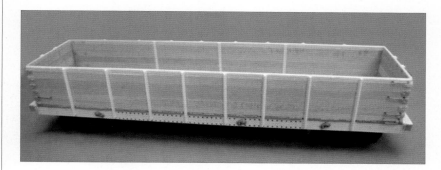

Mass production can save time for scratchbuilders as well as for commercial manufacturers. Perry Squier used Tichy flat cars as the basis for 32 drop-bottom gondolas for his Pittsburg, Shawmut & Northern, and cut all of the wood pieces he needed before starting assembly.

13

CHAPTER EIGHT

Tips from the masters

1

With several important exceptions, what you've read up to this point has largely been based on my own experiences or tips and techniques I have picked up from others. Now I'd like to share some comments from those whose modeling prowess—especially their ability to do quality work in a relatively short time—I have admired over the years. After reading their reports and seeing photos of their results, you'll understand why.

Doug Tagsold strives to have his model railroads—and he's built several of them in three scales—operational in the first year of construction. He also uses scenery techniques that support rapid progress. His multi-deck 1:72 Colorado & Southern reached this state of completion in about two years.
Doug Tagsold

Doug Tagsold:

Over dinner, a group of us was discussing working on our layouts. When my good friend Dex Decker mentioned that he wanted to "do his very best" at building the various structures and scenery for his HOn3 Rio Grande Southern layout, I replied that my philosophy for layout building has always been "to do my very most, rather than doing my very best."

Following looks of surprise and confusion, I explained that none of my models are of contest quality, and only a few might be considered as accurate models of a specific prototype. I said that it's fine to invest the time to do one's very best work on a few key structures or pieces of rolling stock if they are signature pieces. But if one's primary goal is to build a fully scenicked and operational model railroad, he or she probably should not invest that same amount of time and effort into every individual model.

Everyone at the table then agreed with what I had just said. So if you want to complete your model railroad, rather than trying to do your very best, try to do your very most.

I have built and rebuilt four model railroads: The first was an HO railroad depicting the Denver & Rio Grande Western's Joint Line south of Denver to Pueblo, Colo., and the Moffat Road west from Denver through Moffat Tunnel toward Salt Lake City. I then rebuilt the lower (Joint Line) deck to represent the industrial belt around Denver.

The basement of our next-door business building became available, so I built an On3 layout depicting the Denver & Rio Grande Western's three-foot-gauge line from Durango to Silverton, Colo.

Following the sale of our business and a move across town, I built another HO layout, this one a belt line encircling Toledo, Ohio, not far from where we live. Much as my crew and I enjoyed the switching challenges that presented, the siren call of Colorado narrow gauge railroading—this time the Colorado & Southern—and the Rocky Mountains eventually wooed me back to the region I had originally modeled. As I

2

The before and after photos show examples of some of Doug Tagsold's rapid construction methods: a foam roadbed base atop 1 x 3 plywood-framed benchwork, commercial track, and hardboard river bottoms. Inexpensive white bead board used to mock up the scenery profile supports window screen and plaster-coated gauze. That was covered with a 50/50 mix of plaster of Paris and sandbox sand. The hand-carved rockwork was colored with washes of diluted latex paints, ground foam, and real dirt. Envirotex "water" was poured into the creek bed, all in plenty of time for the next operating session. *Two photos: Doug Tagsold*

3 Tom Klimoski models the Georgia Northeastern short line. He got a running start during the lull before layout construction began by having custom decals made and painting and lettering equipment. He also was careful to constrain the overall scope of the new layout to a manageable level. *Tom Klimoski*

4 Tom Klimoski built, drilled wiring holes into, and painted the benchwork for his HO railroad in the garage to reduce the construction mess in the finished train room. Neatness counts, even at the benchwork stage. *Tom Klimoski*

5 Finishing one scene motivated Tom to continue to the next scene, and the next. This also allows testing scenery methods and materials before making a whole-layout commitment that may later need to be updated as new materials become available and techniques improve. *Tom Klimoski*

described in *Model Railroad Planning* 2018, I used HO track but scaled the equipment up to represent narrow-gauge proportions, which came out to 1:72, or about halfway between HO (1:87.1) and S (1:64).

I started the Colorado & Southern in 2014; as of early 2019, the railroad has been fully operational for three years and the scenery is about 40 percent complete, **1**. A lot of kitbashing of rolling stock and locomotives was involved.

So how did I get so much done over a four-year period? Perhaps some of the following recollections and experiences will help you accomplish more in your available time:

Construction skills and methods: I worked summers during my high school and college years for a local homebuilder, so I learned basic construction skills and am comfortable using power tools.

Although I understand the benefits of L-girder construction, I find it to be very labor intensive. I favor box-construction benchwork using ¾" plywood cut to 3"-wide strips.

I use multi-purpose (drywall) screws for fasteners, and I don't pre-drill holes for the screws. I do not handlay track or turnouts, as commercial turnouts work just fine and look "good enough." If modelers want to handlay track, they need to understand that it's going to take much more time.

Goal setting: My number one goal is to build a layout that friends can operate with me. Getting the layout to the point of being operable is always my first goal. Each of the layouts I have built over the past 30 years has been built to the point of being able to host an op session in its first year of construction. From that point on, all construction projects must be completed to the point of not interfering with my next monthly operating session.

The larger projects, such as adding mountain scenery to a section of the layout, **2**, require planning ahead to be sure I have all of the materials to complete the project on schedule. I'd much rather postpone a planned construction project than to start it

Prolific builder Gregg Condon is now enjoying his seventh layout, the Rio Grande Southern in HOn3, as he lays the groundwork for his eighth. He has developed disciplines and techniques that allow rapid progress without sacrificing quality. *Gregg Condon*

and then have to stop while I wait for something I forgot and have to cancel an operating session.

Making good use of available time: I like to keep busy and don't spend much time watching television or sitting at the computer. I spend 15 to 20 minutes each morning reading the daily digest of the previous day's messages of several model railroad chat groups, but I then stay away from the computer while working on the layout.

For various reasons, I have never been a sound sleeper. I often wake up during the night and can't get back to sleep. Rather than lie there for hours tossing and turning, I get up and head to the basement, either to work on some small project or to put in a couple additional hours on a major construction project. Often, one sleepless night leads to a sound night's sleep the next.

I do ask for help from my friends when I need an extra pair of hands, but my irregular and often unplanned work schedule requires me to work alone. If I

Gregg Condon builds almost all of his structures as mini-scenes at his workbench, where they can be rotated 360 degrees as he adds extra detail. Each structure or mini-scene thus receives his undivided attention. *Gregg Condon*

Gregg builds most of the scenery above the track using foam board to establish basic shapes. Below track level, he uses an innovation he calls "clothshell" that allows landforms to be made quickly and easily. *Gregg Condon*

have 30 minutes before I have to go to work, I take advantage of it and work on the layout. I have found myself ballasting track while dressed in a suit and tie before going to my job.

Divide and conquer: Before I start working on my next construction project, I define what it is I want to accomplish, or how big an area I want to work on, and then limit my efforts to that specific task. When building scenery, I like to work on no more than a 10-foot length of layout at a time, and I complete that area to a somewhat finished appearance before I start

planning to move on to the next area or another type of project. Sometimes after working on the scenery in one or two areas, I like a change of pace and choose something different for my next project: building structures or building, painting, and decaling freight cars. A little variety keeps tasks from becoming tedious or even overwhelming, and this promotes progress.

I tend to work in spurts, and when I begin a project, I have a strong desire to see the end result of my efforts. Anticipating the self-satisfaction I will feel when I finish one of these projects

is what motivates me to keep working tirelessly until its completion.

Tom Klimoski:

After we moved, I had about a year and half to plan my next layout, **3**. The planning actually began before the house was even built. When the house was being designed, I determined a space that would accommodate the design I wanted and still provided adequate family space in the remainder of the basement. I also determined that an operating crew of two or three persons would be the ideal crew size

Yosemite Valley modeler Jack Burgess built not one but three models of a brick oil house over the years as more information surfaced. Jack enjoys model building, and by moving ahead with the best information he had at the time, the railroad avoided having a bare spot in a prominent location. He also built the Merced depot twice for the same reason; see **1-9**. *Jack Burgess*

10

Mike Sparks and Randy Laframboise are modeling the Rutland Railroad in the transition era. Randy's decades of experience in construction and project management have taught him best practices to ensure that jobs are done on time, on budget, and to the expected quality standards. *Randy Laframboise*

for me. Once I selected a prototype to model, I was able to do considerable research on it and develop a track plan during that year and a half period.

No prototype models were manufactured for the Georgia Northeastern (GNRR), so I used the down time while waiting to build a layout to custom paint and decal a couple of locomotives for the GNRR. The time before layout construction can be

well spent by completing models that you know you will need. Once layout building begins, those highly detailed and time-consuming projects like custom painting or installing decoders are easy to put off. It's better to complete these projects that don't take up much room but give a layout a more finished look while you have the time.

Our basement was left unfinished when the house was built. I wanted

to finish the basement before I began on the layout. Many would see this time as "wasted," but during this year and a half, I created mock-ups of the benchwork so I could check the depth and height, aisle space, and location of room lighting, all before finalizing a track plan.

I drew the track plan full size on brown wrapping (kraft) paper. I traced around actual Micro Engineering no. 6

11

Randy Laframboise was dreading building a helix and was happy to find a quality kit from Ashlin Designs. In less than 8 hours, the helix was ready for tracklaying. Outsourcing parts or labor can reap a huge time savings. *Randy Laframboise*

12

Randy found that rolling work stations and storage cabinets enable him to quickly get materials and tools to the layout location he is working on without wasting time rounding up what he needs. *Randy Laframboise*

13

turnouts to get the exact locations and angles of the sidings, which allowed me to tweak the design and visualize the full-size plan. It was easy at this point to move turnouts slightly to get a better flow of track or check the length of sidings for adequate car placement. Once I had the benchwork built, this "template" was then placed on the benchwork and the track plan was transferred to the subroadbed.

This also allowed me to plan for the location of depressed areas for rivers and streams. This template saved hours of time once track laying began, as all the bugs had been worked out in advance.

Before the drywall was installed, I added additional bracing in the walls where needed, saving time later. The entire train room was finished and painted with lighting and carpeting installed.

My old layout was in our garage in Miami, Fla. Often it was too uncomfortable to work on the layout. Having a finished, climate-controlled room motivated me to work on the layout.

I built the benchwork for my new layout in the garage, **4**, including painting and drilling holes for wiring. Installation was easy, as all I had to do was attach it to the walls. This saved time while avoiding making a mess in the train room.

One of the benefits of a small layout is that each stage of construction goes relatively quickly. It is a whole different ballgame when you have a total of 21 turnouts to install instead of hundreds. Each task does not seem overwhelming when the amount of work is manageable.

Many times modelers want a large layout, only to find that they become overwhelmed with the amount of work and lose interest. I use the term "right-sized layout" to describe my railroad. Obviously, what is right-sized for me may not be the same for someone else; it all depends on one's givens and druthers. By keeping the layout sized correctly for me, it motivated me to keep making progress and get to the goal of a "finished" layout.

Once I had the trackwork done and wired, I tested it by having operating

sessions. Nothing tests a layout more than a full-scale op session, and I saved a lot of time by discovering operational glitches before scenery got in the way. I used structures from my old layout, cardboard mock-ups, and markings on the subroadbed to indicate industries. Having op sessions motivated me to replace the temporary structures and replace them with scratchbuilt or kitbashed structures replicating the prototypes.

I got the biggest bang for the buck when I completed the scenery in the Tate Yard area, **5**. The scenery in the yard covered a large area and was done quickly, as there were only a few trees and grass areas along the backdrop. Completing this one area really made the layout look more "finished" even though I still had a long way to go.

Once I had the yard area done, I began systematically working my way out from the yard. By working in sections, I was able to complete a scene before moving on to the next.

I tend to work in spurts: I work on a project until it is completed and then take a short break. As I completed a

Low-profile LED lights helped Bernie Kempinski eliminate back lighting on the Falmouth portion of his layout—evident when only the fluorescents were turned on (left). The low air-conditioning duct precluded another fluorescent fixture. Low-profile LEDs, with a simple styrene valance mounted on the lower edge of the duct, allowed better foreground illumination and balanced out the strong backlighting from the fluorescent fixtures behind the egg-crate diffusers (right). Bernie reports a slight color difference between the LEDs and fluorescents, but "it's hard to notice when you're standing in the room." *Two photos: Bernie Kempinski*

scene, it motivated me to keep moving along. By alternating between building structures and then scenery for an area, it broke up the tasks into manageable parts.

The biggest tip I can offer is to have a good idea of what you really want from a model railroad. Having that clearly defined goal will help keep you motivated; lack of motivation is a huge time-waster. I like highly detailed and completed scenes with operations focusing on prototype-based procedures, so having a small switching layout was the best decision I could have made. Getting a layout operational and holding operating sessions as soon as I could manage has proven to be a huge motivator for me to make steady progress on my layout.

Gregg Condon:

When we moved into our current home, the basement was one gray concrete void. After we upgraded it, it took 18 months to build my HOn3 layout, **6**.

I have brought seven room-size layouts to a "photo finish"—my term for a layout that is of publishable quality and complete in all respects, **7**.

Layout five (*Great Model Railroads* 2007) was completed in two years. It filled a 17 x 90-foot room. I surprised myself at the speed of construction; obviously, I had learned some useful techniques. Layout six (GMR 2013) was brought to photo finish in 18 months.

Halfway through layout six, I realized I was building a layout without plaster! I formalized that technique into something I termed "clothshell scenery" (**8**), which became a key point in my layout-efficiency repertoire.

Layout seven (GMR 2019) was brought to a photo finish in 22 months, which included starting with a new

basement with a bare concrete floor and installing drywall and lighting, finishing the crew lounge and HVAC room, completing benchwork for eventual layout eight (I have two side-by-side 17 x 40 train rooms), building the depot-dispatcher's office, and completing HOn3 layout seven to a level that I term "a walk-in museum diorama."

Here's what for me is the most efficient path of layout planning and construction activities:

Know what you're going to do ahead of time: It's terribly counter-productive to have afterthoughts that require undoing something that has been completed. Put the plan on paper if you must; I can see the train room and layout in my head and just build it, so have never spent any time with CAD or pencil.

Make it a priority: How important is a model railroad to you? You don't

14 Dundon, W.Va., on Brooks Stover's Buffalo Creek & Gauley is shown after about a year of construction on his new, and smaller, S scale layout. His timesaving techniques apply to any scale. *Brooks Stover*

15

get something of tremendous value without tremendous effort. Not much progress will be made if the layout is the activity of last resort after everything else has been completed. When building a layout, I'll look at a month in advance and pencil in times—and lengths of times—to work on the layout.

Decades ago, I gave up TV. I made it a foundational part of my character to prefer my own achievements over being entertained by watching somebody else's activity.

I kept a time log and recorded 1,600 hours spread over 22 months. That averages 18 hours a week for almost two years to build my layout. There were weeks when I didn't work on it at all; there were days when I worked on it for 14 hours.

More is accomplished in blocks of time several hours long than in minutes here and there. Blocks of entire days back-to-back are ideal—as in 36 hours in three days. Don't want to do that? No problem; nobody says you must complete a layout in a year and a half. We make choices and live with the outcomes.

Pre-build: On my previous and current layouts, I had all the structures, bridges, and train equipment

completed before I ever set foot in the new train room.

I pre-build what I call "benchwork scenes." Most of the interesting detail seems to be immediately adjacent to structures. So when building structures, I make a scenic base part of the structure and add the details to it at my workbench where the lighting and the posture in my chair are ideal, **7**. As Henry Ford demonstrated, I take the work to the tools. At the workbench, the small scene can be turned so that every angle is accessible. With only one scene receiving attention at a time, best efforts are achieved.

Room prep: I clean out the train room and start with a clean slate. I install ceiling, lighting, and walls. I also paint the ceiling, walls, and floor—and the sky backdrop—before the benchwork is in the way.

Layout construction: I install the benchwork along with the wiring before roadbed and scenery are in the way. In yards, I use ½" Homasote on top of ½" or thicker plywood. [The author recommends ¾" birch plywood. Ted Pamperin built his HO layout on ½" Gatorfoam board.]

I lay and wire the track before adding scenery between the fascia and track. This allows much of the wiring

to be reached from above.

That done, I cut the fascia to shape with a jigsaw and install scenery between the fascia and track. Most of the scenery between the track and backdrop is foam hills, and most of the scenery between the fascia and track is downward-sloping clothshell, **8**.

Jack Burgess:
The Yosemite Valley Railroad, which I model in HO as it appeared and operated in August 1939, had an oil house at its yards at Merced, Calif. The first time I realized it was there was in a listing for the building in the Liquidation Notice issued by the scrapper of the railroad in 1945. The building was for the storage of flammable materials. I finally obtained a photo of just a portion of the brick building. Assuming that I would never get a better photo, I built a model of it based on the size in the notice and that single photo.

I eventually obtained another photo of the building taken during the scrapping operation that showed the side toward the turntable. That photo showed a large window on that end of the building rather than a door. And another photo I obtained several years later proved that there was no door on

Many layouts have to be accommodated in space also used by the family. Following the dismantling of his previous Iowa Interstate layout (left) for basement sewer-line work, James McNab used IKEA shelving components to quickly assemble benchwork for an HO model of the IAIS's Hills Line (above). The benchwork also provides shelving for magazines, toys, and other household items. *James McNab*

the trackside of the structure, either.

Sometime later I got a copy of a California Railroad Commission engineering report for the YV that listed all of the buildings on the railroad and details of their construction. With that additional information, I built a new model of the oil house that matched the photos and other details of the building. Or so I thought.

Years later, another YV modeler was studying the plans that I had drawn for the building and a Sanborn fie insurance map. He noticed that, unlike most buildings, the long sides rather than the short sides of the oil house were "peaked." So I built my current version, **9**.

That first model was built in the early 1980s and the last one around 2015. Along with more prototype information, my modeling skills also improved over this stretch of time.

But during this period, rather than waiting for information that might never have surfaced, I did have a presentable model of the oil house on my HO railroad.

Clark Probst:

Other than depots, I've done only one stand-in structure model. The plan was to scratchbuild all the layout structures in two months' time. I was running out of time for my self-imposed deadline, so I modified a building kit to sort of look like the real one.

By the time it was finished, I figured I could have scratchbuilt an accurate model in the same amount of time. To throw salt in the wound, visitors zoomed past accurate buildings to look at the stand-in, exclaiming, "That's Hoxie Fruit!" Hoxie Fruit didn't occupy the building until well after the time I modeled, so that wasn't a compliment.

After hearing this one too many times, I scratchbuilt a correct model, and no one mentioned Hoxie Fruit again. This taught me not to use stand-ins.

Randy Laframboise:

As construction on Mike Sparks' and my Rutland Railroad layout progressed [**10** and MRP 2016], I was dreading building a helix to move trains between decks. I was delighted to find a high-

quality kit from Ashlin Designs (ashlintrains.com), **11**. In less than 8 hours—far less time than it would have taken with any other method—the helix was ready for tracklaying.

Trying to find a needed tool is a chronic time-waster. I solved that problem by using a rolling cart containing almost everything Mike and I will need to tackle a project, **12**.

[More helpful tips from Randy's vast experience as a professional project manager and model railroad builder appear in the 2020 edition of *Model Railroad Planning*.]

Bernie Kempinski:

Before I started work on an O scale Civil War-era layout in my basement, I installed some inexpensive shop lights and low-profile under-cabinet lights to illuminate the layout. The layout has changed a couple times, but the lights have remained. In fact, I have added more.

But most of these fixtures have failed at one time or another, some more than once. Replacing the under-cabinet lights isn't too hard, but the shop lights are more difficult in that they are over parts of the layout with deeper benchwork. I am phasing them out with smaller fixtures so they are easier to replace. Moreover, replacing tubes over finished scenery is bad enough; replacing ballasts is even more difficult.

About two years ago, I started switching to long 4000K LED light strips to replace several of the problematic fluorescents lights, **13**, as I describe in my blog (www.usmrr. blogspot.com). Thanks to a tip from Frank Hodina, I ordered an 8-pack of Sunvie LED T5 Integrated Fixtures from Amazon. Combined with some 18"-long 4000K LED light strips I got from Home Depot, I was able to greatly improve the lighting in my layout room and shop. Better still, these lights are supposed to last 50,000 hours.

The LEDs also use less power, create less heat, do not emit much UV, produce a consistent light color, and are linkable, making wiring much simpler. These fixtures are also lightweight; I used hot glue to install them. I was able to put them in locations that help avoid the back lighting that my existing light system created.

Brooks Stover

My S scale layouts have depicted the Buffalo Creek & Gauley, **14** [see *Model Railroad Planning* 2019]. I am part of what I call a mutual admiration society of eight S scalers who share thoughts, opinions, and encouragement. All of us have layouts in some stage of construction, and several are very far along. For whatever reason, however, few S scale modelers actually get layouts completed.

In an effort to encourage S scale modelers to build complete layouts, we recently pooled our thinking on the subject of how to get a model railroad built. I wrote an article on the topic for the National Association of S Gaugers *Dispatch*. Here's a quick summary:

Do something every day. It's possible to make progress by doing at least one simple task each day—place an order for a part or tool you'll need for an upcoming project, pick up a

16

quart of paint thinner when you're at the hardware store for a household project, drop an email to a modeling friend seeking advice on a modeling technique, or make a simple note or sketch of an idea for your layout.

Stay focused. While at first "focusing" may seem like a constraint, in reality having a clearly defined prototype (or well-defined reference prototype for a freelanced railroad), specific geographic location, and a carefully focused era will ensure that every piece of rolling stock, each structure kit, and every scenery item you purchase will be usable on the layout and not sit on a shelf.

Consider the layout and its environment together. A model railroad is piece of art, the visual expression of its creator. Taking the time and expense to finish the railroad room's ceilings, walls, and floors pays big dividends by focusing all the viewers' attention on the layout itself as well as making it comfortable for

visitors and operators.

Keep it simple but challenging. A model railroad is a complex entity made up of many elements that must work in harmony to be successful. Every effort toward simplification will pay big dividends in construction and maintenance for you and for operators.

Don't try to do it all. Take full advantage of ready-to-run or "plug-and-play" products and technologies that can greatly speed layout construction. For example, use quality commercial flextrack and turnouts instead of handlaying track, and add a few details to a RTR car instead of scratchbuilding.

Build in cycles. Constructing a layout by completing all the benchwork, followed by all the wiring, then track, then structures, and finally scenery might be efficient, but that can lead to getting burned out during one of those phases. Instead, complete one section of the layout before moving on to the next.

Jeff Hallion screwed the benchwork frame into pre-stained IKEA Ivar shelving. He built everything in sections to make it easy to make changes by removing the top from the shelving uprights and to disassemble the shelving units. Tubs on the shelves will make storage easier and neater. Jeff plans to add a fascia so the final look will be something similar to what David Barrow has done on his most recent layout. *Jeff Hallion*

Embrace standardization and consistency. While it's always good to be aware of new products and techniques, there are big advantages to standardizing on aspects such as couplers, wheelsets, decoder brands, and even scenery and paint brands.

Maintain a well-stocked inventory of supplies and tools. Having a good inventory of "consumables" on hand such as standard wood, plastic, and brass shapes and strips, adhesives, knife blades, drill bits, and paint will ensure you'll have what you need for that one-evening project that you just got the inspiration to build.

Clean up after work sessions. Allow a few minutes at the end of each work session to put everything back in its place so you'll know where everything is when you have time to work again and resume the project. And keep each active project in a suitable container so the entire project can easily be brought back out the next time you are ready to work on it.

IKEA components
The last two reports concern using IKEA shelving kits to save time and effort.

James McNab:
One of the key goals for my new layout, The Hills Line, was to allow the layout room to serve as a secondary family room. This meant designing a space that would be warm and inviting for my wife and son as well as meet my needs for an operating model railroad.

I discovered that other model railroaders, notably Bernie Kempinski (see **4-2**, **4-3**, and **13**) and Marty McGuirk, had used IKEA's Ivar shelving units on their layouts. The modular units allow for a quick and straightforward construction process that can adapt to a variety of configurations. The Ivar product also offered far greater quality at a lower cost than I could build using similar-quality lumber.

I quickly painted, stained, and assembled the shelves in our basement, then built a modified L-girder top to support the railroad itself. While I was limited to the shapes and sizes that are available from IKEA, I was able to use individual Ivar components to create a more customized solution for our space. Primarily I used the 12"-deep by 31.5"-wide version, but also used shorter lengths to fill in the spaces around the room. Since the layout is 16" deep, standardizing on 12" units allowed for a toe space at the front of the layout.

The Ivar units are primarily designed for utility use and are neither ornate or intricate. That allowed me to attach the L-girder directly to the leg units, speeding construction. Leg levelers were added to the bottom of each shelf due to the unevenness of our basement floor. The Ivar units are not attached to the walls, but the L-girder top connects each individual shelf into a continuous and stable structure.

To finish off the space, commercially available literature racks were combined with Ivar leg units to produce the look of built-in storage for my collection of hobby magazines without the cost of custom benchwork, **15**.

Jeff Hallion:
Using IKEA Ivar shelving is really pretty simple, **16**. The frame is screwed into the Ivar shelving, which I had stained.

I built it in sections, so if I ever want to move it or change out a section, I will just remove the top from the shelving uprights, pop apart the shelving units, and am good to go. I'll put tubs on the shelves to store stuff, which should keep things a bit tidier.

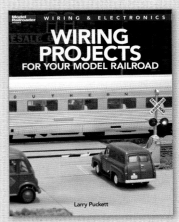
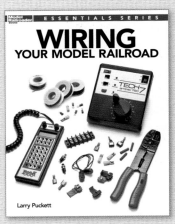

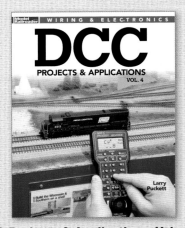